Tempus ORAL HISTORY *Series*

Filton
voices

D1198935

A Methodist church Sunday school party in the mid-1950s.

Tempus ORAL HISTORY *Series*

Filton
voices

Jane Tozer and Jackie Sims

TEMPUS

Bristol Type 171 Sycamore helicopter, developed at Filton, first flew in 1949. The Helicopter Division moved to Weston-super-Mare.

First published 2003

Tempus Publishing Limited
The Mill, Brimscombe Port,
Stroud, Gloucestershire, GL5 2QG
www.tempus-publishing.com

British Library Cataloguing in Publication Data.
A catalogue record for this book is available from the British Library.

ISBN 0 7524 3097 1

Typesetting and origination by Tempus Publishing Limited
Printed in Great Britain by Midway Colour Print, Wiltshire

Contents

Acknowledgements

We would like to thank the many people and organisations contributing to this project. First of all, the participants, who so generously gave their time and shared their memories and photographs with us. We are grateful too for the generosity of the South Gloucestershire Aviation website (www.aviationarchive.org.uk), part of the 'Three Centuries of Transport' project, who have generously helped us with funding and technical issues, and who will in turn be using some of our oral material. Thanks go to Jon Poole, our interviewer, who undertook the project with cheerfulness and skill. Recognition also goes to Ann Tee and Pat Giles of Filton People, a local voluntary group, who helped with the task of editing the interviews for this book. Finally we must not forget the Community Fund, Awards for All, whose grant made the project possible.

Acknowledgements are due to the organisations who have generously allowed us to use photographs: Airbus UK, BAE Systems, Rolls-Royce Ltd, Bristol Cars, the *Bristol Evening Post*, the *Western Daily Press*, the *Gloucestershire Gazette*, Filton Camera Club, Filton Town Council, Marchington Fire Service, Mr and Mrs R. Hall for the use of the photograph of Severn Beach, Sydney Marks for his photograph of Tom Walker, Joan Dando for her Cabot souvenir programme, Hobbs Chemist's for photographs of his shop.

Grateful thanks go to the following who have generously contributed to the project: Bristol Aero Collection Museum at Kemble, Betty and Peter Beardmore, Mr Baker, Frances Blandford, Tim Bowly, Arthur and Dorothy Breens, the family of Mr A.W. Britton, Glenys Buckley, John Buckley, Sid Chilcott, Ann Churches, Tony Crook, Filton Library, Mr and Mrs G., Walter Gibb, Ken George, Mike Goose, John Harris, Audrey Hawes, Rodney Hewett, Eden Holder, John Hutton, Irene James, Sylvia Johnson, Mike Jones, Charlie King, Phil Kirley, Mary Lake, Frances Logan, Sid Lovesy, Maureen Lomas, Sue and Geoff Lonsdale, Sydney Marks, Roy Mockridge, Audrey Monks, Pat Paice, Cliff Price, Colin Pulsford, Mrs R., Thelma Ryczko, Hilda Saunders, Philip Shield, Toby Silverton, Stan and Jackie Sims, Phyllis Sutton, Robert Talboys, Margaret Tarr, Jane Tozer, Keith Trott, Ms W., Kristine and the late Maud White, Dennis Wiltshire.

Every effort has been made to identify the copyright holders of the photographs in this book, but we apologise to anyone overlooked in our search, and to photograph owners, should they be omitted from the list.

Finally *Filton, Gloucestershire* by W.L. Harris has been an invaluable resource during the whole of this project.

Introduction

The development of the aviation industry represents the single largest factor in Filton's change from a small rural village on the outskirts of Bristol into a fully fledged conurbation. The growth of Filton has been almost entirely aviation led. Founded in 1910, the British and Colonial Aeroplane Company became the Bristol Aeroplane Company in 1920 and grew to be, at the time of the Second World War, the world's largest aviation production site of its kind. Post-war, the British aircraft industry contracted, with many mergers and consequent name changes. The Bristol Aeroplane Company, Bristol Aero-Engines, Bristol Siddeley Engines, Bristol Aircraft, British Aerospace and many others are now names in history. Today, BAE Systems, Airbus UK and Rolls-Royce (Bristol) are still nationally important industries.

Until the early 1900s Filton was a quiet agricultural village built on both sides of the Gloucester to Bristol turnpike road, later the A38. In 1901 the population was 461. Clustered around the church were cottages and two farms, with other farms in the environs. The rest of the land consisted of ponds and lanes, with fields growing various crops. From 1869, Samuel Shield's laundry on the top of the hill gave employment, along with the farms, pubs and the next-door Phillips' wheelwrights business.

It was the coming of the tramway in 1908 that began Filton's development. Near the Filton tram terminus motorbuses were built and garaged to serve the outlying rural areas. Sir George White took over these sheds and started constructing aeroplanes. The Box Kite flew in 1910, the beginning of a long line of famous Bristol aircraft which included the Bristol Fighter, the Bulldog, the Blenheim, the Brabazon, the Britannia and Concorde. The aviation industry led to an expansion of Filton, culminating in a population of over 12,000. Housing replaced all the farms, fields and ponds and changed the appearance and character of the village forever. About a third of Filton parish to the north and northwest was sacrificed to the aircraft industry. The development of the ill-fated Brabazon aircraft involved the destruction of the village of Charlton, razed to allow the extension of the runway.

In 1963 the Link Road (A4174) dual carriageway completed the division of Filton, already split in two by the A38, into four separate parts.

Although much of Filton's physical past has been knocked down or swallowed up by developments, traces of the medieval agricultural beginnings of this little town are still to be found in road and district names, for instance Glebelands and Warren Road. Some of the farm buildings are discernable beneath later uses – Conygre House, and the Galleon club. The names of prominent residents are commemorated in roads such as Wades, Mackie, Gayner, Shellard, Pilkington, Roycroft and Bridgman. The aircraft industry has provided its own input – Braemar Avenue, Brabazon Road, Canberra Grove and Blenheim Drive.

It was because of the wealth of earlier history now lost beneath urban dwellings that a Community History Project, funded by the National Lottery, was instituted in 2000 to capture and record what is left. This project now includes two oral history collections.

Filton contains a large percentage of older people, and the importance of capturing their memories of a time already past became imperative. In this second collection, over thirty people shared their memories with us, and it is their voices that we will hear in this book.

The personalities of our interviewees comes over through their speech; some colourful, some forthright, but all vividly remembering the taste and texture of the past.

The diversity of recollections covers both the pre-war agricultural community and the industry-led growth of housing and employment. People's sense of loss emerges, as the old order changed and daily life became faster, more stressful and noisier. Their sadness as their rural surroundings were gradually eroded is apparent. The village is remembered as a close-knit community of caring neighbours and friendly shops. School experiences and childhood games and activities are also described.

On the other hand, we have recollections from those who worked in the aircraft industry in various capacities, including apprentices, with accounts of the industry's space programme. The development of the fast, élite Bristol car is recalled, and there are some recollections of a record-breaking test pilot. Many people have memories of the war years, with its deprivation and constant raids, and the way Filton residents nevertheless managed to make their own entertainment.

Some of our contributors remembered their working days in detail. We hear about working in the laundry, serving meals to BAC management, working in the offices and workshops of the aircraft factories, and a site fireman's day, as well as delivering to a butcher's shop, working in the post office and working in a pharmacy.

The original minidisk recordings of the oral interviews have been made into CDs. It is intended that these should be available for private listening and research by local historians. Meanwhile, it is hoped that this record of personal memories will help younger generations to understand, and the older generation to relive their past, while expanding people's awareness of Filton as a town with a rich history of its own.

These are personal memories and the editors cannot vouch for the accuracy of statements made by individuals.

Jackie Sims and Jane Tozer
Filton People Community History Project.

1 A Rural Village

Many of our contributors remember the farms, together with the old way of life, and have seen the fields gradually encroached upon by building and industry. The last farm on Filton Hill closed around 1950. Many people remember the open fields, woods and countryside, and the freedom to roam and play in a way that is unthinkable today.

Trams

The tram cars used to go up there and stop, then pull the old whatsitsname [pantograph] down [the arm that attached to the overhead electric cable], at the Plough, opposite the works entrance.

Phillip Shield

Erratum: the caption on page 9 should read: Five generations of Shields. Phillip Shield, aged 91 with his niece Maureen Lomas, her daughter, grandson and great grandchild

Fi... *e with four generations of his family.*

Playing trams

If mum had to go into town for things we went on the trams. I loved it. I used to save all the tickets, and dad, when he came home on leave, made me a little metal thing to hold the tickets. Very often, me, Jean and a couple of our neighbours' children would play conductors or conductresses out in the back garden, and they'd all sit in a line and one of us would issue the tickets.

Phyllis Sutton

Farms

Pat: Opposite, on the other side of the church, which is now Church Road with the flats, were two farms.
Hilda: It was one big farm with a lot of outhouses.
Pat: Cows, chickens, all of it. We used to have these cans of milk to deliver to about five or six houses. Just below these outhouses that belonged to the farm there was this little Methodist Church up there by the old tin hut.
Hilda: It was very dilapidated, the old church was, but the tin hut was called the Reading Room, and you'd have the Brownies and the Guides in there. Then it got made over into what we always called the Greasy Spoon. Got made into a café. And then down at the back of them was what they called the Withy's, another lot of old cottages.

Hilda Saunders and Pat Paice

A real farmer

Up by Filton Church was the farm. It wasn't a massive farm, but it was a farm. There was also one down at the bottom of Filton Hill, down near the Rodney works. That was Saunders Farm – he was a real farmer, in more ways than one. In dress, you know – leather boots up to here, corduroy trousers, what I would call plaid sort of waistcoat, hat on his head. You couldn't mistake that he was a farmer.

Phyllis Sutton

The cows' daily journey

Where Elm Park is, that was all farming ground. The cows used to come out from the cow sheds where the shops are at the new

The Green Café, formerly the Reading Rooms, with Filton's first Methodist church on the right and the 142 bus waiting at the terminus. Taken from one of the houses on the Conygre Road/Station Road junction before the Church View flats were built in the 1960s.

Church Farm, opposite Filton church, probably in the 1920s. Church House and the employment office are now located on this site.

Shield Centre. They'd come across, stop at the pond along the way for a drink of water – there was also a well there, and then they could go up as far as Ferndale Road or they could go up and turn right and go over to the A38. During the war there was a lot of wheat grown there, quite an acreage of it.

John Hutton

Dead Man's Orchard

On the corner of Blenheim Drive was an orchard– we knew it as Dead Man's Orchard. I've no idea where the name originated.

Cliff Price

Church Farm

My mother first came to Filton about 1932. She used to go to the Methodist Church where the Church View flats are now. It was a tiny little church that was a scout hut when I was young, and next door to it you had all the old Church Farm buildings. They were used to house the local fire engine. The old farmhouse was a huge building, four storeys high. We used to climb through it when we were kids. That's where the labour exchange is now.

Ken George

Helping out

At the top of Shellard Road they built some new houses. In front of the houses there used to be a massive great wheat field. All the local children used to help the farmer cut the hay and go chasing field mice and rabbits.

Rodney Hewett

Farmer Alfred Hutton and his sons stacking sheaves on their Station Road Farm, about 1930.

Haystacks

There used to be a nice row of trees up Braemar Avenue. I can remember the avenue, we moved in 1929. All the bottom of Kenmore was fields. They used to grow hay there. They had a haystack on the corner of Dunkeld and Rannoch Road and the boys set fire to it. There used to be another one, I think, at the top of the hill at the top of Kenmore. There was a wheat field over on Monks Park school playing field. The egg-packing station came later, during the war.

Mrs G.

Changing times

We've lived into the space age. I used to say to my father 'You've lived through a wonderful time.' We had no radio before the war. When father bought his first radio he was so proud, and he said 'Well, yes, I suppose so,' but if you live through an era you don't really recognise what's happened, you have to be able to stand back and look at it. I had friends who were in

2152 Squadron in Filton, it was just a village and now the whole conurbation has spread out; incredible how the city grows all the time.

Keith Trott

A sense of loss

I just feel that they're taking all the beauty away from Filton and it's becoming a concrete jungle.

Phyllis Sutton

Sledging

Margaret: When Mum was born Filton was tiny.

Frances: They used to have wonderful times in the snow when she was younger. Before they built Conygre Road up, they used to climb to the top of the hill there and get sledges and tin trays and what have you, and slide down the hill right to Conygre House. There were big gates across there and she said you often got hurt because you'd smack into the gates. There's just so much traffic and it's ruined with that Link Road down through the middle.

Margaret: People needed the work. That's why Filton grew so big really, to house the BAC workers I suppose.

Frances Logan and Margaret Tarr

Time moves on

I suppose we have to progress, we have to go forward. It was hard to accept. My biggest blow was when Lloyd's Bank (formerly Laundry House) was pulled down. I could not see why that beautiful building had to be destroyed. They are also trying to get Conygre House. We rallied round and a few of us went up and protested to Mr Lucena, who's retired now but had been the clerk for so many, many years. He put in a very strong letter about pulling that building down. Somebody from Thornbury Council gave us a lot of feedback.

They wanted it for development and the house would need such a lot done to it, but we knew it had a new roof and it's had numerous things done to it. It's been brought up to a standard for even the council people to work there, so it cannot be as dilapidated as they are trying to say. But Filton House I did think should have been kept as it is and used as a museum for the people of Filton. It would be lovely for children to know the history of Filton.

Thelma Ryczko

Childhood illnesses

My sister Jean spent two years in hospital with diphtheria. Scarlet fever was rampant in those days; so was tuberculosis. Unfortunately she was a germ carrier of diphtheria; she didn't get it as bad as the ones she gave it to. She put four other relations in Mangotsfield Isolation Hospital.

Conygre House in 2001; until the 1920s there was a farmhouse here, built on the site of Filton Manor.

We couldn't go in the room where she was, you had to speak to her through a glass partition.

Phyllis Sutton

White House Café

I lived in my family home in Filton Avenue. We used to walk across a bit of wasteland where the houses are at the bottom of Station Road up through Wades Road. At the top there was an orchard. There was only the church there then. I can remember going there as a kid to Sunday school. There was a great big tin hut and that's where we used to go to Sunday school. Years later it was turned into some sort of a café for workmen. Right where Taylor's the estate agents are, that used to be called the White House Café. We once went to a wedding reception there. All the BAC workers used to go in there for their lunches.

Sylvia Johnson

Walks around Filton

Where the MOD there used to be two woods. We used to go picking bluebells and primroses. They are now protected species, but we used to go over as children picking bluebells by the armful and making little posies to bring back to our mum. There was a big farm there; we were allowed to use the footpath. Going past the farm there was another little wood with a footpath, and that brought us out to what was called Duchesses. We used to have picnics, and go fishing for tiddlers.

Phyllis Sutton

Nature walks

One of the things I remember from my junior school years was the nature walks; walking along Golf Course Lane and the teacher pointing out old man's beard and telling me that its proper name was clematis. I can also recall an incident when I walked into the

The White House Café, c. 1950.

The Rank, a row of late-Victorian cottages opposite Filton House, demolished in the early 1930s to make way for the rank of shops, including Boots.

farmer's field where the present playing fields are. There were some cans that had been thrown out. I picked up one of these cans and a little bird flew out. I realised that a robin had nested in the tin. Birds, robins in particular, nest in peculiar places!

Cliff Price

The Rank

While I was going up and down to school, the BAC started building their big new Filton House. Opposite this was the Rank.

These cottages had no back entrance so everything had to go through the front of the house. If they had a horse it had to go through the front of the house because they couldn't take it round to the back.

Audrey Hawes

Phillips the wheelwrights

The old cottage I told you about behind the flower shop Sabrina Vallis – that must be very

old. That was Tom Phillips'. He was part of Phillips the wheelwrights and they used to make wheels for the gun carriages which went to the Boer War.

John Hutton

Carved up by the Link Road

Before the Link Road, all the traffic wanting to go to Avonmouth would have to come up and go along between the churchyard and Church Farm. Coming out of Bristol, anything wanting to turn right for Filton, Frenchay or Downend, places like that, would have to turn right where the golf shop is at the top of Filton Hill.

John Hutton

'Them and us'

Margaret: They cut Filton in half by doing that dual carriageway.
Frances: The playing fields got cut in half, and we lost the Memorial Hall. That was a good

On the corner of Station Road is part of the former Church School, replaced by Charborough Road School in 1927. The building was then used for church activities and demolished in 1954 to make way for a new church hall.

Station Road, site of an ancient lane from Filton church to Frenchay, was so named when the railway came to Filton in the 1860s. The houses on the left were demolished in the 1970s to make way for the A4174 dual carriageway.

function place. It was quite sad, it just didn't seem the same after they put the Link Road, as they call it, in. So you got 'them and us'.

Margaret Tarr and Frances Logan

Link Road and traffic

We literally sold our house in two-and-a-half hours because the buyers' house was being pulled down to make way for the Link Road.

There was a whole row of I don't know how many houses, which is now on the left hand side if you go down the Link Road. The traffic is chaos now, whereas it used to be so quiet. Twenty, twenty-five years ago you could walk up the road and go to church. You didn't even need to use the zebra crossing because there was no traffic then. Now even on the zebra I nearly had my skirt taken off the other night. Cars stopped, I had the green man, I got to the middle and all of

The Memorial Hall, built in 1926 adjacent to the laundry, on land given by Samuel Shield. It was at the junction of Gloucester Road and Southmead Road, and was demolished to make way for the Link Road.

a sudden a motorbike came and my skirt whistled in the wind!

Ann Churches

Anchor

The memorial hall stood opposite what was then the Anchor pub, which is now the Mill House. That was where everything took place – any sort of social function, the local drama group, everything met there. That was pulled down. There was a post office on the corner that had been there for years that had to go, for the Link Road to go through. They put the big roundabout in which is still there to this day.

Audrey Hawes

Road changes

One of the big things is the road system changes. At the moment it's just carved up by dual carriageways, and that is one of the biggest changes in Filton. It's carved Filton up into four quarters; the quarter for the Works,

the Charborough Road area, the Third Avenue area etc., and an area the other side of Station Road.

Ken George

'The Steep'

My brother and I were born up at our relations place – Lane's Dairy. We moved down to 7 Station Road in the 1920s. There were loads of fields. What is Mayville Avenue now was all fields there, and we always called it the Steep because if you know Mayville Avenue it's a very steep road. There was a big house at the bottom of the road on the corner with lovely fruit trees we raided regularly. That's where we always played. Mum would come to the bottom of the garden, just call our names so we could hear her, and then it was time for a meal.

Hilda Saunders

Hilda Saunders with her sister Pat Paice and a friend, in Station Road by the church, c. 1930.

Apple orchard

Halfway down Filton Hill on the right-hand side was the farm belonging to Farmer Saunders, and he used to deliver the milk in churns. He had the old apple orchard. We used to climb over the wall and pick apples and get chased. The one thing I remember most was the area at the back of his farm that you could reach from Station Road. My parents forbade me ever to use it but because I was forbidden to use it of course I felt I had to. It was called the Steep, and we used to go down the Steep, which was fine. But when you got to the back of Farmer Saunders' land, he had geese, and they were worse than any guard dog. They would really attack you if they had a chance.

Audrey Hawes

New homes

I can't believe the buildings that are here now because we were literally on the edge. We were really in the suburbs when my parents came here in 1937. There wasn't even a pavement. The bus only went to Wallscourt Road and it was all a mess there.

Sylvia Johnson

An early bathroom

We all moved in from older properties, like us from Shellard Road. These houses in Conygre Grove were enormous, with an upstairs bathroom and indoor toilet. We had an outside toilet at Shellard Road, and the bedrooms were upstairs, and that was it. Then you had your living room, fireplace and back kitchen, and off the back kitchen was the bathroom. The bath was served by a gas boiler which mum had to heat up for you to have a bath. There was a tube leading from the thing into the bath, and from the side of the boiler she pumped water into the bath.

Margaret Tarr

Jennings the builder

When we came all the buildings were done, finished, in Northville Road. W. Jennings was the builder, and he lived opposite in the bungalow there.

Mrs R.

The Avenues

We came, first of all, to Sixth Avenue in 1928, waiting for the Seventh Avenue houses to be built. This was part of the Jennings Housing in Filton; the Third, Fourth, Fifth, Sixth, Seventh, Eighth, Ninth, Tenth, and Eleventh Avenues.

Ms W.

A view of the airfield

Number 18 Victoria Park was a house rented from the railway company. We had a front room which was for very special occasions, a middle room, a kitchen and a scullery on the ground floor. Going up between the front room and the middle room was a staircase; no windows or anything, just a staircase that went up. There was a front bedroom, and you had to go through a middle bedroom to get to the little bedroom at the back that looked out over the airfield. We used to look out through that back window and see all those old aircraft, the Bulldog and the Moth and all those things, taking off.

Audrey Hawes

Moving from Hotwells

My father moved to Southmead in 1924 because of the congestion of two brothers working in a small space in Hotwells. My grandfather decided to come out one day for a ride in his car and he came to Southmead. He saw an existing garage for sale and bought it. It cost him £600. It involved the building and an acre and a quarter of land behind, and this was at the time a farming community. Each day he came up from Hotwells on his motorcycle to Southmead to open the garage to serve the customers and he went home on many an occasion without even seeing anybody – 'not even taken a bean', as he said. He had to come up through Bridge Valley Road, across the Downs, Henleaze Road past the Manor House at the bottom of Southmead Road to work. He had to open and close many gates on the way, which were involved with the various estates in Henleaze and on the Downs. From there he developed, and eventually in 1931 had a bungalow built where the family grew up.

John Buckley

John Buckley with his grandparents Charles and Harriet Buckley in 1935. Charles Buckley bought the garage on Southmead Road in 1924.

Growing up in The Plough

I can remember when my dad kept the pub The Plough. I used to crawl on the floor and drink from the drip tins, and the dog did as well and we got drunk. That's why they had to shoot him in the end, I think. The Westmancotts had The Plough after my dad.

Phillip Shield

Shops

There was Trevelyian's the hairdressers on the end. It's a chip shop now and I can't remember what was next door up. Then you

The Plough, when Phillip Shield's father was licensee, c. 1915. Who was 'Raffles'?

had Mrs Plunkett, a tobacconist with a few sweets. I remember her mainly because I had to deliver the meat there, and she was a right one. She'd poke it around: 'what rubbish do you call this?', and give me a right telling-off. It was nothing to do with me; I didn't dish it up. When the Works closed for holiday fortnight she closed. She wasn't interested in customers in Filton. She got all her money from across the road at the Works. There were grocers and all in those days. I remember that during the war we used to have a cardboard box full of groceries. My father used to pick it up on the Friday and that was our groceries for a week. It measured fourteen inches by ten to twelve inches, and included a 100 cigarettes for my father.

Ken George

The old fire tender

Pat: Next to The Plough, Miss Evans ran a newsagent that's still there now. Next door to that was Hodge's. There was a shop there then with vegetables and things. Then there was a rather nice house.

Hilda: Opposite there was another old house, a shop and at the back of that were some cottages. The fire bell was there, and you had to climb the wall to ring. The fire brigade had a truck; they had to push it, it wasn't very modern, and they used to run with it. Then when that went they had the fire station in a big old shed in Church Road, and they had a proper fire engine then. We used to live up in Station Road, and there was a lane going around the back. Next to the lane there was a big driveway, and there was a big bungalow there where Mr and Mrs Long and their daughter Peggy lived. He had a garage at the top of Filton Hill and he was there for years. Next to that was the police station, then it was Lane's Dairy, then next to that was Turner's the bakers, then next to that was a bank.

Hilda Saunders and Pat Paice

More shops

Molly lived in the bungalow opposite me. Her father kept a hairdressers and I can remember vividly that people used to queue outside to have their hair cut. There were seats inside, but they were right out along the front of the other shops queuing to have their hair cut. There was a shop that sold everything. In those days it was called a haberdashery, and she sold buttons, children's clothes, women's clothes, and all the normal underclothing for a woman, and children's dresses. There was a grocery shop, Mills', and there was Turner's Bakery.

Phyllis Sutton

Old-fashioned service

I remember what was nice about the provision shop Robinson's. My eldest daughter used to take my brown bag, bought the stuff and it was all packed and everything. Take it or leave it now in the supermarkets, you've got to grab it quick and get out the way.

Mrs Breens

A 'front room' business

Maud: Mrs Bird's shop in Hunter's Way, she'd get stuff, bring it back, and she'd put it on the counter and she perhaps only had three of these items and you'd see it and say 'Oh my God that's just what I've been looking for.'
Kristine: She enjoyed her little shop. It was the front room of her house turned into a shop, and it was there for many years and it did provide a good service.

Maud and Kristine White

Northville Market

Northville, where I'm living now, was built in the 1920s, but before that people have said the whole area was just fields, and it gradually got built up and up. The shops at the top of the road here had everything. We had a cooked meat shop, a little delicatessen, a home-made cake shop, Foot's Fancy Goods, International Stores, Peark's Stores, a Co-operative grocery store and shoe repairs. You didn't need to go to town to shop because it was all on your doorstep. This was called Northville Market, and it was a little market where you could get whatever you needed. Sugar was sugar and it was just one standard price, and tea was tea. You didn't have to shop around. Things were seasonal, and when the war was on, things like tomatoes you could only get when they were in season. I can remember queuing with my mother and pretending not to know who she was so that she could go in and buy a pound of tomatoes and I could go in and buy a pound of tomatoes. We had to pretend we didn't know each other.

Audrey Hawes

Ice cream

Opposite the pub, the King George IV, was a shop called Damond's, and through the war we used to queue up for ice cream. They only used to come once a week, on a Thursday. I remember distinctly that it was an absolute treat to have an ice cream on a Thursday.

I can remember there was a shop up at Filton Church and it was called Ali Baba's. It

Joyce Taylor became Children's Librarian when Filton Library moved to the vacant Methodist church in 1959 and opened a children's section.

sold absolutely anything and everything, and the chap was there for years and years and years. I think it's where Bakers Dolphin is now.

Sylvia Johnson

The library moves

We moved in spring 1959 to the new building, which was the old Methodist chapel. The original idea, before the Link Road was built and the roundabout put in, was to build council offices behind the library for the rural district. The Methodist chapel library would have been one wing. The library did have a junior section for the first time.

Frances Blandford

New job for the post office!

When the old post office was dismantled for the Link Road to go through, part of the old building was sold to a gentleman who became my next-door neighbour. He built a garage in his garden from the old post office!

Cliff Price

Extra post office activities

I actually started cookery lessons in the post office. We had a gentleman come in one day; he'd been widowed three weeks, and I said 'How are you?' He said 'Alright, but it's the food.' I asked 'What's wrong with the food?', and he said 'I'm living on sandwiches.' He said he was frightened of the cooker, and that he couldn't put anything in the oven, so I jotted down a couple of things that he could get at the butchers that he could grill, and I started him off grilling. I told him to come back in half an hour when my queue had gone down and I'd teach him what to do. And I did. This was in May. By September he was going to night school at Monk's Park.

My boss used to help the widows, because some of them had never had a bank account, signed a cheque, or even got a joint account with their husbands. He used to do the forms and things for them. So we were a friendly post office. We used to have people coming in from Chepstow, Almondsbury, and Thornbury; they worked in this area and came to us because we were so friendly.

Ann Churches

A small house in Hunter's Way

Kristine: There were two rooms down, a front room and a kitchen. Then upstairs you had two bedrooms and a boxroom.
Maud: Nothing much – you couldn't even get a bed in it. So we bought a new bed and had some of the base cut off. It broke my heart to think that you had to pay all that money for the bed and then have it sawn off.

Maud and Kristine White

Filton Park

Mrs G.: Do you remember Uncle Tom's Cabin up there? It was a transport café.

Mr G.: It used to be Osborne on the corner, the ironmongers, No. 1 Braemar Park (Filton Park). Uncle Tom's was where the car park is now.
Mrs G.: The mortar mills used to be behind that. Don't you remember the mortar mill where they used to grind up all the mortar? Where the flats are now, behind Braemar Crescent. It was only a small sort of shed, and you could hear them crunching up all the ashes, or whatever it was they made mortar with. Brittons the builder used to go round there and get the mortar. It's a shame we don't think to take photographs when it's all about at the time.
Mr G: No, not at the time, no. You were rich to have a camera then.

Mr and Mrs G.

Mushrooms

My father used to come off duty at six o'clock some Sunday mornings. He'd take his mac off and pick mushrooms, and come home with his mac inside-out, full of mushrooms from the fields at what is now Parkway Station and Abbeywood, all that sort of area. You caught a

Filton Station with its three platforms in May 1975. It has since been replaced by Abbey Wood Station.

Cliff Price in 1949, aged nine.

train from Filton Junction. The rest was just fields and woods. You could go and pick primroses and cowslips. That was half the fun of my childhood, just wandering.

Audrey Hawes

More mushrooms

Go down Filton Road from Horfield. As you come to the shops by Braemar Avenue, you turn down left down to Southmead Road. I went down there once and found some mushrooms. I sold them to the local bloke who used to come around with a cart selling apples and pears.

Phillip Shield

Ponds in Filton

One of the big things that changed in Filton from when I was a kid was that we had ponds everywhere. We haven't got any now. In the corner of the field which is now flats on Shellard Road there was a pond. We used to go skating on it sometimes when it was frozen. Where Church Farm was there was a pond at the bottom of the orchard, and a little pond that was constructed for fire use during the war, so that was three ponds that we had to play in. We had quite a population of newts, which are almost extinct now. Before my time there was a pond where the Mill House is now, on that corner.

Ken George

Playing in the fields

There was one place that I used to play a lot, and that was where Filton High School is now. That was farm fields, and there was a stream which started where the MOD is now, a little stream which wound its way across Station Road, across New Road, into the fields where the school is now, under the railway embankment and disappeared. That is one of the tributaries of the Frome. We used to play alongside that river and catch sticklebacks, and just play in the fields. The fields were not used for grazing or cultivation; it looked as if stone had been dug out of the ground in that area.

Cliff Price

The winter of 1947

I can remember the absolutely bitterly cold winter of 1947. It was freezing and the snow was so high. We used to go tobogganing out over Duchesses. We didn't have central heating; we just had one fire in one room. We

Sylvia Johnson in 1948, aged thirteen, with her brothers and sister.

did have a hot water back boiler but apart from that you only had your coal fire in the one room. Oh it was freezing. I used to feel sorry for my mother. There were four of us, my sister was too young at the time to go out tobogganing, but me and my brothers did. We used to come home and all our clothes would be soaking wet, and you didn't have washing machines or tumble dryers or anything. She used to have these great big wooden airing things all round the rooms, trying to get all the clothes dry. All the winter, gosh, it was horrendous.

Sylvia Johnson

A narrow squeak

The winter of 1947 was a very, very hard winter, hardest of my lifetime. We had about eighteen inches of snow. Then it thawed a bit and then froze again, so we had a crust of about an inch on top of the snow that you could walk on. Then it snowed another foot on top of that. At the time I was going to Charborough Road School, and I'd walk up Station Road, across the field, and down where the Methodist Church is now to Charborough Road. I was going across the field one morning and suddenly the ground just opened and I went through it. Somebody had left an inspection cover off and some bracken had been across it and supported the snow, and I went straight through the lot. If I'd broken my leg I'd still be there but I managed to clear the snow away and get back onto ground level again. I was on my own right in the middle of Filton playing fields.

Ken George

Filton floods in 1952

There was terrible weather in 1952; we had awful floods. I remember them using a boat underneath the railway bridge.

Mrs Breens

Reg Lane, on the right, delivering milk to his cousin Les King, holding the jug, during the 1930s.

Delivering milk in 1929, with the slogan 'For Health's Sake Drink Hutton's Sunshine Milk.'

'Pea-soupers' in Filton

I can remember several times coming out of church after evensong, and there being such pea-soup fog. We had to walk right down that hill to get home again; my father would go in front and we'd hold hands in a line and follow him because you couldn't see more than about ten or twelve inches in front of your face where the fog was so thick. Everybody had coal fires and there was all the pollution. Quite often we've come down the hill line astern to get home safely.

Audrey Hawes

Walking home through smog

I can remember that we had very bad smog and you couldn't see in front. I can remember walking home from Gloucester Road and I couldn't see one foot in front of the other, it was absolutely petrifying. I remember walking to work and walking home and I thought 'I'm never going to get home.' It was that bad, the weather.

Kristine White

Home delivery

I can remember the farmer coming around with a cart with milk churns on it. You didn't get your milk in bottles; you had to take a jug out and get your milk jugs filled from the churn, and that's how your milk was delivered. Everything else had to come the same way. The coal man called, the oil man called. We had no electricity – it was all oil lamps. There was no central heating, and in the winter if you took a glass of water to bed with you, by the time you woke up in the morning the water was frozen in the glass and the windows were scaled with frost on the inside. We had a kitchen with a scullery area at the back with a coal-fired boiler. You had to light the fire under the boiler, a big stone thing, and you'd boil up the water and get enough hot water to have a bath. The big oval tin bath hung on a nail outside the kitchen door, and that was brought in and you were bathed in front of the old kitchen range. The toilet was outside. You had to go out through the back door, down a little way, and turn down a little lane bit and the toilet was there, so that was another cold job in the winter.

Audrey Hawes

The late 1940s

Margaret: It was great, it was lovely. Everybody knew everybody in Shellard Road and Mackie Road and all round there. People babysat for each other so we had loads of aunties that used to babysit for mum.

Frances: And we could just go out couldn't we? Go out all day over the woods.

Margaret: We had this old claptrap bike and we used to ride up and down the road.

Frances: Went as far as Severn Beach when we got a bit older.

Margaret: The old Anderson air-raid shelter in the garden – mum grew nasturtiums all over that. She threw loads of seeds and she had chickens in the back garden and our grandmother lived next door. We lived at No. 5 and she lived at No. 7 Shellard Road.

Frances: In between Shield Road School and Brabazon Road there was an ash path. There were bushes each side and allotments one side and then the little stream. They still call it the ash path, but it's tarmac now.

Frances Logan and Margaret Tarr

How travelling around Filton has changed

There were no cars. The most traffic you got was when they were going to work at Bristol Aeroplane Company on that main road, and that was only in the morning and the evening. My father didn't have a car until just before I got married, and that was in 1956. We had the

Sisters at Christmas, 1949. From the left: Margaret Tarr, Frances Logan and their sisters Beth and Pat.

Tommy Walker, gentleman of the road.

television just before the Coronation. You didn't have those sorts of things when we were kids. It was just a real, real luxury to have a car, absolutely fabulous to have a car. But you could travel about.

Sylvia Johnson

Tommy Walker – gentleman of the road

Margaret: Tom, when he was around, was lovely.
Frances: With his bike, he was around for years and years. He was bushy, rather hairy.
Margaret: Never do harm to anybody.

Frances: He was a lovely man.
Margaret: I think he went to Winterbourne Centre in the winter.
Frances: But he was around for years and years.

Frances Logan and Margaret Tarr

Sharing

He was always around Filton, and I can remember sitting with him one day and sharing his dry bread when I was a kid. He was lovely. He was well known in Filton. I can remember him one day giving me a penny; when I look back now I bet that was all his money. He used to like the children. I used to sit on the wall at the King George pub and chat with him. He had a long beard and everything. He was all dirty, but he was a lovely person.

Kristine White

Hand-me-downs

Tommy Walker – he was an old character of Filton. He was from quite a wealthy family, but for some reason or another he took to the open road, he liked his freedom. His two wheeled bike I can remember vividly. He used to decorate the wheels and his handle bars with coloured raffia. His hair got ever-so long and he used to sort of wind it round and push it up under his cap. Very often Gran would say 'Tom, I got some shirts, go out in the back, have a wash, I'll have your others, and they can be thrown away.' Uncle Dave often used to say 'I bought myself some new trousers, I've got a couple of pairs that will fit you, put a clean pair on, and others can be slung and here's a spare pair to put in your haversack.'

Phyllis Sutton

Gipsies

Margaret: There were gipsies up the back.

Frances: We never really had any trouble. They used to come round with their pegs and their wax flowers and there was one my mum got friendly with.

Margaret: She used to tell her fortune.

Frances: Everything she told our mam was right. I was the youngest of four daughters, and she was expecting another one, and the gipsy just looked at her and said 'You're going to have your little boy this time,' and she did. She used to come in every time she came round to have a cup of tea.

Margaret: With her lucky heather.

Frances: It was the wax flowers I can always remember. Paper made with wax.

Margaret: They were sort of a family. Part of the community really. Never thought anything different about it. At Gipsy Patch Lane there was a gipsy community down there. There were gipsies at Stoke Gifford. My great-grandmother lived at Stoke Gifford and was like a midwife for the area. She wasn't trained, only by the doctor, but the gypsies would only let her go in when they needed their children delivering.

Frances Logan and Margaret Tarr

Prefabs: the height of modern living

Remember those prefabs? Our Auntie used to have to keep the ice lollies in the fridge. A fridge was a luxury in those days, and a built-in boiler was real luxury. Our mum used to have to go out to use our old boiler to do her washing, and then she'd go out the back and get the old mangle, the old wringer out, and that was the way we washed years ago.

Kristine White

The home of the stationmaster of Filton Station, the last prefab to be demolished in the 1960s. The Filton prefabs were produced by the Bristol Aeroplane Company's Housing Division at Weston-super-Mare.

Sylvia, aged thirteen and with her cousin on her knee, wearing her Chipping Sodbury Grammar School uniform.

'I can't imagine my life anywhere else but Filton'

I can't imagine my life anywhere else but Filton. I go out now to the shops and I never go where I don't meet someone to talk to. I could pop out for five minutes and could be gone about an hour I'm talking to so many people that I know. When he was small my grandson used to come in and say 'Grandma, you know everybody!' It's because you live in that area and there's a fair few people that have lived here all their lives like me. You've got a lot of memories to talk about then. It's quite nice really.

Sylvia Johnson

2 Schooldays and Apprenticeships

Filton's first church (later national) school outgrew its church buildings. A new school opened at Charborough Road in 1927, an adjacent secondary school following in 1934. Shield Road Primary School opened in 1938 and Filton Hill Primary in 1954, while Filton High School opened in 1959. The BAC Apprentices College on Filton Hill opened in 1955 and Filton College in 1961. Filton Avenue School on Lockleaze Road in Bristol opened about 1930, and included a secondary school.

St Peter's Church School (c. 1926)

I couldn't have been terribly old – about five or six. I went to the church school opposite for just a short while. In the cold winter months mum used to bring my brother and I a hot drink, but she was stopped from doing that. We were very privileged really, because it was just at the top of the road. It was only a stone's throw.

Hilda Saunders

A school group in 1926 outside Filton Church School. Hilda Saunders is sixth from the right in the second row. Her brother Sid Chilcott is third from the left in the front row.

Travelling to school

I can remember going up Hunter's Way and up Wades Road, and then up round where the old farmhouse was, and the green tin hut up on the top run by the Verger of St Peter's Church as a little café for many years. I can remember having to go up there to go to Charborough Road School. I used to hate this long trek, and I was four years of age!

Kristine White

Walking the dirt road

I was twelve or thirteen because I was still going to school at Filton Avenue Senior School. I used to walk all the way down Filton Avenue from Wades Road and I enjoyed it. There were no pavements there then, it was a dirt road.

Roy Mockbridge

Coaching to grammar school

I used to travel to Chipping Sodbury Grammar School by coach– there were probably four coaches– one started at Severn Beach and stopped by Northville, and on Filton Avenue, then the George and then out to Chipping Sodbury. Some went via Downend or through Winterbourne and Iron Acton.

Cliff Price

A long walk

By the time I was five I had to go to school, and the school was at Charborough Road. I went all the way up through Victoria Park and all the way along the main A38 until I got to Charborough Road. I had to do that journey four times a day in the beginning, up to the school, back down home for lunch, up to the school again and back home afterwards in all winds and weathers, snow and ice, frost and fog, the lot.

Audrey Hawes

No room on the bus

The bus service in Patchway when I started school in Charborough Road in 1938 was only a single-decker from Thornbury. I used to go down the bottom of Callicroft Road to get this bus to Filton, and of course it was full up and just used to sail through. I used to run home crying, because if you didn't go to school that was an offence, and the truant officer was on your doorstep the next day. Things were very, very strict.

Betty Beardmore

A missed opportunity

I was fourteen in October 1935. Mum, being a widow, had allowances for us three kids, and the day I was fourteen my mum took me to school to get the headmaster to sign the pension book to say that I was staying until Christmas. At the beginning of December the headmaster, Joe Thompson, called me out and gave me a letter to read. Foot's had a fancy goods shop up Filton Park, and were asking if he knew of a girl that was leaving school and would like a job there, especially if she could leave ready for the Christmas rush. I took it home and showed it to mum, and she said I couldn't leave because the pension book had been signed for me to stay until whatever day we were going to break up, so I never got the job at Mr Foot's. I ended up at the laundry instead. I think I always wanted to go in the laundry because a lot of my friends were there.

Hilda Saunders

Apprentice toolmaker

My father got a job at BAC in about 1937, and we moved to Filton. We lived at Wades Road. I went to Filton Avenue Senior School where I graduated from in 1938. My mother knew the boss of the tool room at the North Filton Works, and he got me an apprenticeship as a toolmaker. I was very fortunate. I started at the BAC in 1939, and had a very good learning there. They taught me a lot, which helped me when I went to the United States. I had no trouble getting a job.

One time I was making a slingshot out of silver steel, which is very expensive, bending it in the vice, and then all of a sudden 'pow!' the foreman hit me alongside the ear. I had to spend two days on the 'surface plate' straightening out that silver steel. I've never forgotten that. He said, 'You're going to stay right there until that ruddy thing is straight again.'

The guys would have fun with apprentices. They would say, 'I want you to go and get me a sky hook from the store, the tool crib.' I would go over to the tool crib, and he'd say 'Well you tell them we've just run out.' The left-handed screwdriver was something else they sent me for. The tricks they'd pull on apprentices! They'd have a block of hard steel in the vice, hardened steel, and they'd give you a file and they'd say 'I want you to take the corners off of that block,' and you'd file, and all you'd hear was grating and scraping. Then the foreman came along and gave them a bad time for doing it to me. But I had a very good apprenticeship there with the BAC.

Roy Mockridge

Shadow factory apprenticeship

I started my apprenticeship in 1944, at a firm in Wiltshire, Marine Mountings. At the

Betty and Peter Beardmore on a tandem in 1951, outside 51 Callicroft Road, Patchway.

cessation of hostilities, the firm just closed down. It was a wartime firm, a shadow factory type of thing. My father managed to get my apprenticeship transferred to Bristol. I did five years' apprenticeship, starting at nineteen shillings and sixpence a week. I've still got it on my indentures now. I was in the tool room; I didn't actually work on any particular engine. We used to make the jigs and fixtures for the engines to be bolted and worked on, drill jigs and all sorts of things.

Peter Beardmore

Aeronautical apprenticeship

I could have gone to the Works straight from Staple Hill on a machinist apprenticeship. As it was, I went to college, came back and went as what they called an aeronautical apprentice, where you were destined to end up in the drawing office. I went for an apprenticeship after college on 13 July 1953, did five years and

Number 2 shop at Bristol Aero Engines Ltd, where Peter Beardmore worked, c. 1953.

finished up in the drawing office designing drilling tools.

Ken George

Electronic instrumentation apprenticeship

Bristol Siddeley Engines were the first people to come up with an interview, and the first people to come up with a job offer. I started off as an apprentice there, so part of my time was at the technical college at the foot of Filton Hill, which is now Filton College. I did workshop training there, learning all the different techniques. I remember the fun of welding aluminium – you had to be very careful because it starts to go into the soft state if you leave the torch on too long, and you create a big hole. It was always a source of great pride, or a bit of luck, if you could weld aluminium. I can remember we also had the Vulcan flying test bed by Barnwell Hall, and they had a bit of a disaster because the turbine

blade sheared off through the engine, ignited the fuel, and the Vulcan caught fire. Fortunately no one got hurt, but a brand new fire engine was lost.

At that time I was staying at Barnwell Hall, on the edge of the airfield. It was run by the YMCA and was used for first-year students and apprentices, so it gave them a stable start in Bristol before letting them loose in the city. It probably wasn't as threatening as it is now, but I suppose coming to a big city they wanted to protect them. I think they wanted to get a feeling of community among the apprentices. So after that, it was a case of a sandwich course, six months at university, and then six months doing the rounds, test beds, drawing offices. It was about £3 15 shillings (£3.75) per week. My mother and father had to help me out, because I think it was something like £3 a week to stay at Barnwell Hall, leaving me 15 shillings a week. And it cost me to go home to Swindon on a Bristol bus every weekend.

Tim Bowly

Apprenticeship at Bristol Aeroplane Company (Engines Division)

My father started at Bristol Aeroplane Company just after the First World War. He worked for Bradley Straker, bought by BAC to form their Engines Division. Father knew Roy Fedden, Engine Division's chief engineer, and got my two brothers apprenticed. I remember my mother had to pay £10, which was a fortune, to get my eldest brother away from St George's Grammar School. If she hadn't got him away before he was sixteen, he wouldn't have gotten his apprenticeship.

My younger brother was in the jig and tool drawing office, starting there about 1936 when he got his National Certificate, but he did night school at Merchant Venturers, which was really quite an achievement in those days. My father made him up a drawing board and a case, and he cycled down Denmark Street or Unity Street to the Merchant Venturers' place to get his qualifications.

Betty Beardmore

Learning the aircraft trade from the bottom up

I started in 1952 as an apprentice, aged sixteen. It was £1.50 (30s) a week gross – by the time stoppages were taken out it was about twenty-four shillings – £1.20. I was always broke. When I came out of the training school, the first aircraft I worked on was the Bristol Freighter, working with a gang doing final assembly. I moved down to the flight sheds working on the Brigand, then moved to what was known as the Brab Hanger; now the

The original Bristol Aeroplane Company Apprentices School on Filton Hill was constructed from Bristol Aeroplane Company (Housing) prefabricated buildings. This picture was taken in 2000, before it was demolished to make way for Filton College.

Barnwell Hall was named after Frank Barnwell, designer of the Bristol Fighter, the Bulldog and the Blenheim, and BACs chief aircraft designer until he dies in 1938. The hall was part of a complex of RAF buildings, now demolished. They are on the left centre of the picture alongside Hayes Lane, which met the Gloucester Road at the junction with Gypsy Patch Lane. Hayes Lane closed around 1930. The A38 runs right to left across the picture, above the three hangars which became the BAC Engines Division in the 1920s.

assembly hall. As an apprentice, you would be with a skilled fitter and perhaps a mate, and you had to learn the business right the way through. One time you'd be working on the undercarriage, another you'd be doing sub assembly, making up parts, skinning the aircraft, then final assembly, fitting out the interior. You just moved from job to job as required. Moving from section to section you got a thorough grounding in the entire business and the industry. I was the company's top apprentice one year, and I ended up in research, which was always considered a plum job. For starters you weren't on bonus and you tended to get more interesting problematical jobs to do, and I stayed there. I think one of

the biggest changes is that in those days, you learnt to handle any job connected with the construction of aircraft. Now, as in all jobs, they've become more specialised and compartmentalised, and people know a lot about a little whereas we were good all-rounders. You got thrown in at the deep end. In 1954 I'd been working for the fitter and we were putting in the very first engines in the first production Britannia. He went down with flu, and there was nobody else who knew how to put the engines in. The foreman came up and said 'If I give you a gang of labourers can you put the engines in?' I said 'Yes.' For an eighteen-year old you thought 'God, this is brilliant.' People had a terrific

Mike Jones, top fifth year apprentice in 1957, receiving an award from Sir Eric Ashby, Vice Chancellor of Queens University, Belfast. The award ceremony took place in the BAC Canteen on Southmead Road.

pride in their work – whenever an aircraft took off on its maiden flight, everybody stopped work to see it fly, and you'd think 'my department did that.'

Mike Jones

Joining BAC as a fireman

I served my apprenticeship on the railway as a painter on the civil engineering department. In 1963 I joined the auxiliary fire service as well. I served my apprenticeship, got my City and Guilds, and then Dr Beeching came along and a lot of us had to go. As I was in the fire service at Bristol, I thought I'd go in full time.

I was tall enough, but didn't have the chest measurements laid down by the Home Office, so I couldn't go in. Our training officer said they were looking for firemen at Filton. I applied, went to the interview and medical, got the job and stayed there twenty-eight years.

Robert Talboys

Apprenticeship at Hobbs' Pharmacy

I did my apprenticeship with Percy Hobbs at 544 Filton Avenue, which took two-and-a-half years I think. The first year I earned five shillings a week, the second year seven and six

Robert Talboys in a close proximity suit used for rescue work, always worn during Concorde testing in 1968/69.

Day release

I went to BAC at the age of fourteen. I was interviewed, got a job, accepted and was told I could go to day release classes at Bishop Road to learn bookkeeping and shorthand typing. I started as a sort of runabout doing filing and things like that. After about two years, the secretary to the chief inspector left to get married, and I was the only one in the department that had shorthand and typing skills. I took her job and was secretary for the chief inspector for about eight years.

Audrey Hawes

More day release

I started as an office girl, and then I was allowed to go one day a week to the Merchant Venturers' training place in Unity Street in Bristol. I was a good typist. I thought a typewriter was the most wonderful thing I had ever seen. I picked up typing but I could not get the hang of shorthand. I had a friend in the office who was absolutely pie-hot at everything. She could sing, she could dance, and she could play the piano. She was absolutely wonderful at everything. Mr A. allowed her to go to day release and she picked it up, but I didn't. So he said to me 'I can't allow you to go anymore, Miss Pearce, you're wasting the firm's time.' But because my friend picked it up, Mr A. said to me 'If I allow you to go again, will you promise me that you'll try harder?' I went to Bishop Road and I picked up the shorthand then.

Betty Beardmore

a week, and into the third year ten shillings a week. I was apparently so helpful that Mr Percy Hobbs kindly gave me twelve shillings and sixpence a week. It was very low – it wasn't a wage you were expected to live on. If you were serving an apprenticeship, you were learning and he was teaching you. I went to pharmacy college on the top two floors of the Merchant Venturers building just off Park Street. I spent two years there, qualified, and my first job was managing a shop at No. 13 Gloucester Road North. Bristol Chemist Ltd it was called, about 1947.

Ms W.

Hobbs' Chemists on Filton Avenue, about 1950.

A BAC typing pool in 1948.

3 Growing up in Filton

Organised youth activities were not lacking in Filton, both during and after the war. The Methodist youth club came under the leadership of Alfred James in 1941. The club included successful sports teams and a drama group led by Mrs Irene James. There were Air Training Cadets, Sea Scouts, Scouts, Guides, Cubs and Brownies and sport and activity youth groups.

Methodist Youth Club

The youth club started, I think, in 1940, in a shed at the back of what was then the Methodist church. I joined it when Alf and Renee James were running it. I must have been about fourteen then, I suppose, and it was good. We had a small half-size billiard table. We played billiards, not snooker. We had a couple of table tennis tables, and a dartboard in a little room on its own. We'd go down there Tuesday and Friday nights. At the end of the evening, about ten o'clock until half past or quarter to eleven, the tables were cleared away and we had a gramophone on. We had a bit of dancing – ballroom, strict ballroom dancing in those days. The youth club also did a lot of drama. They did exceptionally well with Renee James as producer.

The Duke of Beaufort, seated front centre, visits his own Filton Methodist youth club in Charborough Road, in November 1956. Irene James is in the chair on the right-hand side and Alfred James is behind the Duke.

Filton Methodist youth club play tennis against Stoke Gifford in 1950. Irene James is fifth from the left in the front row with her son David beside her.

Alfie James was a guard on the railway, and used to sit in his guard van trundling along on goods trains at night doing all his paperwork for the youth club so he was able to keep the two jobs running. Tragically they were killed on the A38. Nine children and Alfie. That shook the whole community.

Ken George

Filton Methodist Youth Club

Mrs James: We came to Filton in 1941 when my husband was moved because of his job. He worked for LMS Railway, and then of course he came into youth work, full-time youth work.

The Methodist youth club started in 1941; it was blackout, and the boys and girls didn't know what to do with themselves. We immediately set up a youth group. We started with a small number, a very small number, and then the bigger place was built and we were able to expand. Some of them have moved abroad and Christmas time's a lovely time because then I hear from all these people.

At first it was in the little room at the back of the church. We just had a group of boys for a start, and then the girls wanted to join. Of course, the war was on, and the blackout, and the parents worried about them coming out. But times were very different then to what they are now. I've seen very big changes in young people.

Glenys Buckley: The headmaster allowed you to use the secondary school hall. We got on very well with the headmaster there, and his wife.

Mrs James: We had a lot of interests. I set up a drama group first. I was very interested in the drama. The girls played hockey and netball, and the boys played football and all the games that could possibly be played. Table tennis and billiards, that was very popular, and when the summer came there was a tennis court up at the top and we used that. At first we didn't have a tennis court. We were always very keen on tennis and our children were beginning to grow. We were driving down Woodlands Road, where Bradley Stoke now starts, and we used to cycle through there. A lady lived

In 1967 the Reverend Arthur Shaw laid the foundation stone of the new St Andrew's youth club, in the presence of the youth club's head boy and girl and church leaders.

Cowley Manor, Cheltenham, where the youth club spent some weekends. Gloucestershire Council had purchased the manor from the Horlicks Company, who left their butler and other staff thus ensuring a wonderful service.

just along there, and we got talking to her. She said 'I've got a tennis court in my garden that I never use, if you'd like to use it.' I said that would be lovely for Saturday afternoons. 'Well, you're very welcome,' she said, so we came to a very good understanding. She used to allow us to borrow the kettle in the kitchen and make a cup of tea. If you take people in the right way you get treated in the right way in return.

Glenys: When the Charborough Road Centre

was opened in 1941 we went in there. And then eventually the church was built, and they built a youth centre behind the church. That was in 1968 in Elm Park.

Mrs James: We went to all sorts of places, and we had some wonderful times. There were several places in South Wales that we went to. We helped build Biblins in the Wye Valley. We went there quite a lot, for long weekends.

Glenys: We helped to build it.

A newly built Charborough Road Youth Hut in 1941.

Mrs James: Over two years. We had proper builders to guide us. It was lovely to think the young people could take a hand in it.

We spent many weekends at Beverstone near Tetbury and Cowley Manor near Cheltenham, and weeks. In fact, we had a group of Germans come to stay with us, and they spent a week at this place. And Severn Springs – that's another bit of Gloucestershire. We did games, and going for walks, and especially sitting talking – we spent a lot of time talking to them.

We always had a members' committee. We thought it was very important that there should be a youth committee as well as a leaders' committee. They used to love to become members of the youth committee when there was room for them. And it worked very well that way. The Young People's Committee and the leaders worked together, and this is how the programmes were sorted out.

There was a stipulation about joining. They just couldn't walk in and then walk out, they had to make up their mind whether they were going to be interested in the youth club. After so many weeks they could become real

members. They really wanted to belong once they heard what was going on. They liked all the different games they played; they liked all the interest. We went out and about a lot with them, that was the thing. We spent some wonderful weekends away with them, and they had to know that they had to behave themselves and pull their weight.

We used to have a group of club members that came to church every Sunday night. To have a group of young people coming into church regularly on Sunday night was quite something. After church most of them came to our house, before we had the youth club built. We were in Conygre Road then, so they knew that they could come in if they sat on each other's laps! We loved it. My husband and I loved young people. We tried to do the best that we could for them at the time. The parents were worried about them coming out in the blackout, but once they knew that they came there, that they came in to enjoy themselves after church in another room, they got used to the idea.

To celebrate the new church at Elm Park we had three weddings! The couples met in

43

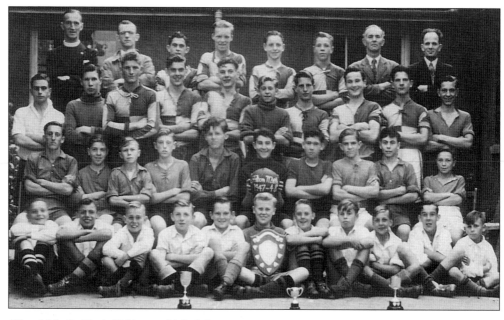

Filton Methodist Youth Club's successful football teams in 1947. Rod Hewett is in the front row holding the trophy.

the youth club and they eventually married. When the new church was built they all decided to get married at the same time.

Glenys: There were lots of young people who met at the youth club who got married after, but these three were made a big thing of because it was all on the same weekend. It was almost like a dating and marriage bureau!

Mrs James: It was obvious that the club was very successful and they wanted to be part of it, and no matter what you asked them to do, they would join in and do it. They really were very committed young people. They didn't have the alternatives of going to town like they do today. They never went to town, it was unheard of. Everything was concentrated in Filton in the youth centre. There was always something going on. Then we had the annual dinners, and the annual sports days. We would transport everyone out to Iron Acton by coach. And they'd come back for a sit-down meal and concert in the evening, all prepared by youth club parents.

Glenys: During 1947-48 we won five trophies in the Gloucestershire football competitions. We won the five-a-side football. I can't remember them because I wasn't involved in the football team. There's a lovely photograph of all the boys. You had to have them standing on benches, and parading them down so that the younger ones were sitting on the floor. It was taken in Charborough Road School.

Mrs James: Table tennis was very popular. We had three tables at one time, and they had to put their names down for their turn. That was one of the most popular things. There was the Stewart Grainger trophy, they called it.

It was surprising what an interest people came to show in what we were doing, and then they picked up the idea of giving a trophy for this that and another. We had a lot of trophies at one time. Netball was very popular with the girls.

I ran the Drama at the youth centre, and loved every minute. They were all good drama plays. We didn't write them ourselves; they were all books that we'd read. There was quite a bit of comedy, and general interest. *An Air for Murder, Haul for the Shore* – that was a popular one. It went on until we finished. I retired in 1968.

Glenys: And you became the first Youth Leader Warden at the new youth centre.

Mrs James: I was appointed by the education committee. A lot of our young people had done work with Sir John Hunt and they'd been abroad for about two weeks. My son was one of them; he used to love the adventure side of it. They were going to Cheltenham to meet Sir John Hunt again, and to receive their awards for what they did. I didn't go with them that night because we had a couple of guests from abroad – we were sorting out another youth exchange. I had a cold and my husband said 'Don't go, Renee, stay in with Annaliese and Hans and go to bed early.' Well, I didn't go to bed early – I went to bed the next morning!

There was an accident and we lost eleven people, it was terrible. I don't know whether you know the road to Gloucester – there's one short area where there are three lanes. Well, somebody went into the same lane as we did, and we lost eleven people in a minibus, and my husband. It was a tragedy, because they were the cream of young people. They were going for their awards; they were part of the National Endeavour.

Glenys: They had to do a lot of things to get that award. They had to work, like the Duke of Edinburgh's award scheme.

Mrs James: That's right. It took a long time to get the Endeavour Award; they worked very hard. It was so tragic – just can't believe it happened. It was so sad for all the families, so sad. But we just had to carry on.

Glenys: With regard to football, my claim to fame was because they didn't have a permanent pitch to play on, they used to be dotted around the area. I used to put my brother in the pram, with two stone bottles filled with hot tea, and walk to wherever the

The Stewart Grainger Table Tennis Shield was won for a second time in 1952. The winning team, from the left: Glenys James, Norman Reed, Valerie Davies, Dennis Cox.

football was being played, ready for half-time, ready to give the boys hot drinks.

It was wonderful. We didn't feel deprived at all; we felt that we were part of something very special, and because of what Mum and Dad were doing we were privileged enough to do things other children weren't able to do. We joined in the activities. My brother came on lots of things when he was really just a little toddler, but he was part of it, and the boys and girls didn't mind at all. They used to look after him as well.

We went on exchanges with the German young people, started by Mr Biffin, the Kingswood Area Youth Leader. He initiated a German exchange with Hildesheim in about 1952. I believe it was the first exchange. The emphasis came from that area to stay over there, and my husband and I were engaged when we actually went to Germany.

He was staying in one village, and I was

staying in another. My father was staying on a farm with a widow, and my mother was staying in another area with my brother, and we thought it was hilarious that my mother and father had to say 'goodnight' to each other and go different ways. That was quite a joke.

Mrs James: We enjoyed our visits to Germany very much. It wasn't only once; we went five times.

Glenys: We were hoping that because we were going over there and extending the hand of friendship, and they were coming back here, that there would be a better understanding. Because it was the young people that went, it wasn't the generation that had been fighting in the war. We were hopeful for better things.

Mrs James: On return visits we could only take two, but there were other people willing to have them.

There was no prejudice with some, but there was prejudice with other people who wouldn't let their children go to Germany. But we didn't want that to go on. We wanted everybody to work together, and it did eventually.

Glenys: I still write to the girl that stayed in our house, and I stayed with her. We still correspond, and that's going back forty years now.

Mrs James: That's quite something, isn't it?

Mrs Irene James and Glenys Buckley

A tribute to Alfred James

Everybody had the greatest respect. I've never known anybody say anything detrimental about my father. He had this good rapport with young people. He just seemed to click –

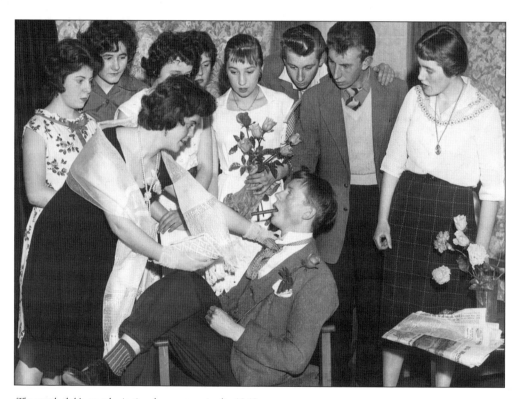

The youth club's award-winning drama group in the 1960s.

The youth club exchange visit to Hildesheim in Germany. Ken George is fifth from left. From the right Alf James is fourth, and John Buckley fifth. Glenys Buckley is seated first left.

he was part of them. He wasn't a leader apart, he was a leader with the young people, and that was borne out by the many tributes that were paid to him at his funeral from all over the area. The church was absolutely packed, people standing all round, and outside as well. It was very touching to see the young men, all dressed in their suits and ties, forming a guard of honour up the steps of the church when the coffin was carried out. I shall never forget, I shall never, never forget, that service, that wonderful church. I felt so proud of my father.

Glenys Buckley

Filton Methodist Church and Youth Club

My mother-in-law, Mrs James, was involved with Filton Methodist youth club; we went to the church when it was up the top of Southmead Road. That's the place where we got married. The original one was a tin kind of building in about 1915 to 1920, which used to be round in Filton itself, down by Church Farm. Sunday school used to be in the afternoon at three o'clock. I always had to go up the road with my brother Timothy, so we used to be charging up the hill. As we came up to the top of the rise, here and on our left -hand-side was the aeroplane Works, and the whole thing was camouflaged, all painted different colours on the brick work. All the

'This is your life' presentation to Irene and Alfred James in 1958. David Sparrow is making the presentation with Brian Powell and Ruth Pope on the right.

windows were open and at three o'clock *Music While You Work* suddenly came blaring out. If we heard *Music While You Work* when we got to the top of the hill we knew we were late!

John Buckley

Some leisure activities

We went to church on a Sunday – there was Sunday school, and in fact I've got recollections that part of that was in Charborough Road School, for some strange reason. There was also the Methodist church, which later became Filton Library, which I used to attend. Then there was the youth club in Charborough Road. The same hall was used for the Cubs. I can remember attending that for a short time.

Cliff Price

152 Bristol Sea Scout Group

I was in the Sea Scouts, the 152 Bristol 1st Filton Sea Scout Group. Their building used to be situated in the corner of the sports field on Southmead Road. Next door to Green Gates there was a bit of land in front of the tennis court fence and the road which was waste ground, and we wanted somewhere to put a scout hut. This would be 1944. We wrote to the BAC saying there was a bit of land by the tennis field and could we make use of it for a Scout hut? They wrote back saying yes. The rent was a one shilling a year 'peppercorn' rent. The parents' committee organised and bought a redundant wooden army hut, which was at Pilning. A few of the fathers were builders, so they went down there and dismantled this wooden hut and built brick piers, and brought it from Pilning and re-erected it.

John Shuttleworth, who lived up in Charlton Avenue, was a commander in the Navy. When he retired he became a schoolteacher. He started the Scout group. Later, George Warder took over. He was part of the Admiralty set up at Bath. At that time we had a government surplus store at Bath, in one of the railway arches underneath the railway station. They had ex-government stock there, brand new and not required because the war was coming to an end. He used to bring back signalling flags, rope, Aldis lamps and all sorts of stuff he considered to be genuinely important for the Scouts. He used to present the bill to the parents committee who were hard-pressed trying to raise funds. He said we had to have it; it's what the Scouts need, which was quite right.

At that time national service was running. Getting people into the Navy, considered to be the premier service, was important, so Sea Scout groups were recognised by the Admiralty as being a potential source of supply. Because of George Warder's excellent leadership we became Admiralty-recognised unit No. 31, giving us access to training on the MTB at Bristol Bridge, and to indent once a year to receive naval stores. Incidentally, we had to pass a twenty-five-yard swimming test in clothing at Bristol North Swimming Baths to be able to go boating on the MTB. We were told not to fall into the river as it was so highly polluted!

John Buckley

Air Cadets

Filton is 2152 Squadron in Pine Grove. We used to go flying on the airfield here; the university air squadron had aircraft called Chipmunks, little two-seater training aircraft. We used to go rifle shooting, and if it was full

Keith Trott aged fifteen, an Air Training Cadet (ATC) in 1944.

bore shooting that was at an RAF range at Pilning. For .22 shooting we used to go Horfield Barracks just up along Gloucester Road. Perhaps a dozen of us would go, and we'd all cram in the officers' cars and drive there. On one occasion there was no transport, but we were going to go shooting. We weren't missing it! Could you imagine twelve boys rushing up Gloucester Road with rifles! We marched from Pine Grove to Horfield Barracks, did our shooting and marched back. The bolts were all taken out and the officer had them in his briefcase and the warrant officer had the ammunition somewhere else. Could you imagine that, they were proper .22 rifles, not kids' stuff!

Geoff Lonsdale

4 Earning a Living

In 1869 Samuel Shield and his wife Mary opened a laundry in Filton, attracted by the plentiful supply of water. This successful business provided employment for many women and some men, continuing until 1951. Other employment included four public houses, many shops, including the pharmacy, grocery and butchers, the post office, two garages, and two dairies. Filton did not lack for personalities; several characters are remembered with affection.

Travelling to work

A lot of people would go to work on their bicycles. When the Works turned out late afternoon it was like the Tour de France, cycles hurtling down Station Road. If we went into Bristol we would always go by tram. Buses took over just before the war started.

John Hutton

Thousands of pushbikes

If you could have seen the Works at 5.30 p.m. it was a sight to behold, because most people cycled. We're talking about somewhere around 20,000 workers all coming out, loads of buses and thousands and thousands of pushbikes going along Gloucester Road, with one solitary policeman on point duty at the Southmead Road junction with the A38, standing and hoping he wasn't going to get his toes run over!

Mike Jones

Bus and train

There was a bus park outside No. 1 gate Rolls-Royce, with designated buses going to Patchway or Gypsy Patch just to pick up. If they were busy, the inspector would be on the main road, and would send the normal service buses in to pick up. Where Rodney Bridge goes over the railway line, there was a halt called Filton North, where they used to run a special train in the morning and at night to Temple Meads. That was an unadvertised service just for Filton and Patchway.

Robert Tallboys

A long train journey

When I first went to Filton I noticed the terrific amount of people commuting to Filton for work. In those days there was a rail station between the runways and the big hangars. Once or twice, I remember, there were bus strikes. I lived near Clifton Down Station, and went to work by train. It went out through Clifton Down tunnel, down the river to Avonmouth, and on beyond Severn Beach, turned in and you got out at Filton North. It went finally into Filton Junction. Mind you, it took about an hour!

Frances Blandford

A 'Green Goddess' from the Emergency Fire Service at Marchington.

Travel by coach

I lived in Kingswood. Although I had a car I preferred to ride on the coach – it didn't cost you any more. There were road changes when they put the new road down through to what is now Abbey Wood. I didn't see much of the biggest change at Filton, more in Patchway and towards Bradley Stoke. That's the way we used to come on the coach. We saw the huge changes, with fields suddenly becoming covered with houses.

Phil Kirley

Working in the Northville post office

Just around the corner there was the old post office. It had a stone floor because it had been a garage. The garage used to house the fire engines, but not the red fire engines. During the war they had fire engines called Green Goddesses in there. I worked in there for twenty years with the stone floor. It was blinking freezing!

Ann Churches

A garage and petrol station (c. 1930)

The petrols we used to sell were Shell, National Benzole, Power Petroleum and British Petroleum. This was served from cast iron petrol pumps with globes on the top to indicate what the petrol was. There was no electricity on site, there was no water and to operate the pumps you had to pump by hand. You pumped it up into a glass bowl at the top, and it was in divisions of half a gallon. You could see when the level came up to what you required. You then put the hose into your tank, turned the hose cock and drained the petrol from the glass bowl into your tank. You then closed the hose cock, pumped up the next half a gallon, and took however many gallons you wanted.

We had sold Shell petrol for sixty-eight years, right up until 1990. Then we signed up with a company called UK Petroleum at Westerleigh, and carried on with them until we sold the business in 1996, when it was demolished. It is now an old people's home.

We used to look after the cars of the Shield family at Shield's Laundry at Filton, and the

Hilda Saunders on the left, with her brother Sid Chilcott and sister Pat Paice, with their mother on her eightieth birthday in 1968.

Bridgman's, who lived in Conygre House and were farming at Harry Stoke. On Southmead Road there are two houses, Green Gates and The Shrubbery. In Green Gates lived a family, and the father worked for Elders & Fyfe, the banana importers. My mother said he brought in this yellow thing that she'd never seen before and said to her 'Would you like to try this? We are importing this new type of fruit with the bananas.' It was a grapefruit, and he said to cut it in half and put sugar on.

John Buckley

Hard work for Mother

She used to do the cleaning up at the Horseshoe public house in the morning. Then she'd come home, have a wash, change out of her heavy work clothes and go back and be a bar maid. Then she'd come home

and go up again at night. She had a very hard time, but she was always happy.

Hilda Saunders

Ivor Jones, the butcher

I was born at Victoria House, next door to the Horseshoe, right in the centre of Filton. At the time it was a butcher's shop run by my uncle. Butchering in those days was somewhat different to what it is now, because not only did he have the shop, he had an old Ford van with half a pig, a sheep and a chunk of beef in the back, and a big plank of wood to chop it on. He went round villages like Patchway, Almondsbury and Stoke Gifford, serving meat out the back of a van, which would not be allowed today. I worked there as an errand boy for a number of years – my only source of pocket money during the 1940s and 1950s. Initially I'd go round Filton with a bike delivering meat. When a chap bought the shop off my uncle, he had a van, and he'd employ a driver. We used to do a round through Patchway, Almondsbury, Stoke Gifford and Lockleaze. It would take from 8.00 a.m. Saturday morning till 1.00 p.m., maybe 1.30 p.m. for which I got five shillings. I'd deliver all weathers, in snow a foot deep. We stopped at Almondsbury sports ground, the van would go off and deliver back into Patchway again, and I'd walk across two fields to deliver one person's meat. I was ten or eleven then I suppose.

Ken George

Developing the library service in Filton

Filton Library was in Northville and adult only. It started two or three years before I went there. It was a prefab building opposite the cinema, owned by the civil defence.

Filton Methodist Church became Filton Library in 1959 when the new St Andrew's Church at Elm Park opened.

They retained a room in the basement with a transmission base. I remember once they delivered a thirty-foot transmission mast. When fitted it had a range of some thirty miles. We had thousands of books. One thing you did not have to do was read a book, though you had to become expert in knowing how to work the boilers!

We had to have new boilers in the Methodist chapel. To begin with it was cold, because they hadn't brought in regulations about buildings in those days, but you thought nothing of it. You put an extra cardigan on. If it got down to 32°F, you kept your coat on. Being used to mobile libraries, I was used to working in those temperatures.

Frances Blandford

Pharmacy inspections

We had a lot of inspections in my day. There were the dangerous drugs; you had to sign for everything that came in and you had to make a note of everything that went out, and that book was checked by the police. You had Customs and Excise come to check the methylated spirits and what sort you kept.

The fire people would come and check where you kept it for fire reasons. People had to sign if they bought anything other than the purple-coloured methylated spirits. You had the weights and measures' people who spent ages balancing the scales. You had the big scales where you sold four ounces of cough sweets, and you had the little scales where you might weigh out five grains of diamorphine hydrochloride or something.

The Pharmaceutical Society of Great Britain always came in plain clothes so that

An aerial view of the Shield Laundry complex, taken in the late 1920s.

nobody in the shop ever thought you were in trouble with the police. The inspector slipped you a prescription – you didn't know who he was – and the next day he would come back and say 'Can I have the prescription for..., I am the pharmaceutical inspector.' He would check, if it was tablets, that we'd given the correct amount, that we hadn't done them down by one, or even given them one too many, which was just as bad a crime!

Ms W.

The laundry

Filton is built on a hill. If you stand at the top you could look in all directions, you're at the highest point. There was a copious supply of water for the laundry, 35,000 gallons a day. There was the pond and the well in the field at the back of the laundry. When prefabs were in

Shellard Road where the flats are now, the woman in the corner prefab nearest the pond always had a beautiful garden even in a hot dry summer, because of water trickling over from the pond. It does seem remarkable that water somehow found its way up to this height.

John Hutton

Working at the laundry

It was a fairly biggish laundry. You had a big area that had the semi-finish, and a bigger area that had the fuller-finish, and then you had the dry-cleaning area. Before we went to school we waited by the laundry for Nellie Phillips; now she *was* Nellie Shield. Mum knew Mrs Phillips from school days, and when we saw Mrs Phillips coming towards us she asked 'Hello Nellie, my daughter's fourteen today. I wonder if I could have her name put down to come to the laundry?' I had a couple of cousins working in the laundry, and they came down and told mum in the dinner time that there was a job for me. When I went into the laundry I was on ten shillings a week. Mum had eight, I had two. I went all through the semi-finish. You put things through what was called the colander. You didn't worry about the crease because it was a semi-finish. But in the fully-finished, if you had a crease on anything, then you had to damp that and push it through so you didn't have a crease. It was properly done. I think I worked on all the presses that were there, including steam presses. I even did the ironing up there, which I must say is a favourite hobby of mine, though you'd get the odd burn. Mr Herbert was in charge then. Mr Ernie saw to a lot of the machinery and the vans, and Maurice worked up in the office. Herbert lived in the house they pulled down. Nellie lived, as Ernie did, round at the top of Southmead Road.

Hilda Saunders

Employment for women

The laundry was one of the main employers of ladies in Filton. They seemed to employ loads of women sorting laundry, ironing and pressing, that sort of thing. I think most of them working in the laundry were married women from Shellard Road; all the ones I knew did anyway.

Ken George

Working my way up

I was fourteen. My first job in 1946 was at Shield's Laundry. I went up and had a little interview, and I worked in all the departments of the laundry. I started doing what I call the most menial things, but they could see I was eager to learn. I liked ironing and washing. When I was first married, everything was done by hand or a little gas boiler. I went through all the departments. I started off in

A Shield family outing in 1910. Ernest Shield is driving with Fred Shield beside him. In the back on the right is Louisa Shield. Mildred Shield is in the centre.

A corner of the office of the Filton Laundry in 1923.

Laundry House, with Mildred Shield standing in the porch.

The laundry sorting room, 1923.

The laundry wash house, 1923.

wet washing, where they had men with big washing machines, and sorting the wet sheets or the wet towels.

The supervisor there began saying 'You're very good, I'm going to start moving you up,' and I went through everything on the presses, even the packing from the end, because there was a lot of contract work from different restaurants that were beginning to open up and wanted all their stuff clean. Even Southmead Hospital sent things before they started their own laundry. In those days there were lots of starch shirts and starch collars; separate collars because men had studs that fixed the collars to the shirts, whereas nowadays the collars are attached. The vicars had dog collars, and they had to have a real shiny finish. There were so many departments. There was dry cleaning there as well. They used to go out and get the laundry from people in a pony and trap.

Phyllis Sutton

Dr Sinclair

SHE 7 is 'Self Help Enterprise'. Some of us started a committee many years ago. It must be thirty-five years.

Dr Sinclair, the chairman, was German. He came to Filton and had been a doctor in Filton for a very long time. When the war started, a lot of the German people that had been here had to be put away in case they were spies or something. The people of Filton loved him so much that they signed petition after petition and got him out. In recognition, he changed his name from Schnitzler to Sinclair.

In my day, before 1971, the SHE 7 used to do lighting plugs. You had to get components in a tray and had to put them together. It was time consuming, but it couldn't be done by machine. It had to be done manually, and it was lovely for elderly gentlemen to feel they were useful.

Ann Churches

Cllr Pilkington lays the stone of the new Filton Folk Centre in September 1966. From the left: Lesley Harris, Cllr Pilkington, Eric Smith, Mrs Pilkington and Sid Hunt.

Mr Harry Pilkington

Mr Harry Pilkington was, when I knew him, an alderman of Gloucestershire County Council. He'd been instrumental in starting the library, and I found out from his obituary that he was behind almost everything else in Filton too. He had been behind the Filton Technical College, originally. He was the humblest of people, and a delightful friend. As a young person I gathered he'd been a close friend of Keir Hardie, one of the founders of the Labour Party. That shows you how old he was when I knew him! Mr Pilkington was Labour, and one of his staunchest friends was Mr Slatter, who had been the personal private secretary to the head of the BAC, and a staunch Conservative. They were the best of friends. I do remember in appearance Mr Pilkington was very short. He only came up to my shoulder, and looked very much like Mr Pickwick.

Frances Blandford

5 Leisure Time

Filton often had to make its own entertainment. After the memorial hall (which stood between 1926 and 1961) was demolished to make way for the Link Road, the community centre opened in 1967 to provide premises and an environment for the development of both educational and social activities. There were also sports clubs. The Cabot Cinema, opened in 1935, is remembered with affection.

A more relaxing life

Life as a boy in those days was very relaxed with few restrictions and little danger. It was not like today with everything and everyone continually under stress and strain. Everything was easy; even through the war it was very easy and friendly. Doors were open, you could go and borrow this and borrow that.

Rodney Hewett

The 'Triangle'; an area of land isolated by railway tracks behind Canberra Grove.

The freedom to play

Margaret: We were lucky I suppose. We had a good childhood and we had the freedom to play.

Frances: We'd go over to the woods; it was just little wood and big wood. You could go over to the little wood in September and come back with a dress full of hazelnuts. You'd tie your belt tight on your dress and put all the nuts down.

Margaret: And the other place we used to go was between the railway lines up over the back here in Conygre Grove. There was a crossing; it was called the triangle. It was yellow with cowslips, and we used to pick them as you were allowed to then. We used to play out here, ropes across the street, marbles in the gutter and all sorts.

Frances: Bonfire night, we'd been building a bonfire for weeks. We'd go over to the woods and bring anything broken back, everything went on it. Huge bonfires they were, absolutely massive.

Margaret: Everyone would pool their fireworks. Mainly sparklers, there wasn't much else available. It was good.

Margaret Tarr and Frances Logan

Dances and drama

Shield Road School's main hall was opened on Tuesdays, Thursdays and Saturdays for a dance. There was no piped music; we used to have a little band that came and played. For about a shilling or 1s 6d you could go and dance until eleven o'clock at night if your father would allow you to stay there that late. My father wouldn't. I had to be home by ten.

Audrey Hawes

Filton Drama Group about 1946. Audrey Hawes centre front, Gordon Eacott front right, Jack Simpson back right with Gwen Davies next to him. Glyn Webb back left.

Dances at the folk centre

Because there was nowhere else to go we used to go dancing at Shield Road. As soon as the folk centre opened it was brilliant because they have a fabulous dance floor up there.

Sylvia Johnson

The Rhythmites

They used to run dances at the memorial hall. The band had an old fiddle and piano and some drums, and called themselves the Rhythmites. You could dance to it after a fashion, but it was a nice hall.

Hilda Saunders

Song and dance

Filton Townswomen's Guild had a drama group that used to meet every Friday afternoon between two and four o'clock. We used to have a choreographer who was one of our group. We had some famous producers – Sally Noble from Bristol, Patricia Matheson and Peggy Delacy Adams – she used to sing with the D'Oyly Carte Opera Company. We used to pay a musical director. It used to cost us £2,000 to put on a performance. We hired scripts from French's in London.

For example, I did *Abenaza* one year, and Alfred Marks had done exactly the same script eight years before in London. We used to very slightly alter the scripts so that Widow Twankey would say that she wanted to move home near to someone in the audience that had a posh house. It'd be marvellous.

Ann Churches

The Townswomen's Guild present Pantomania *1984 – the Charlston.*

Making friends

When I first moved here with a new baby I didn't know a soul. A friend said 'Why don't you go to the Townswomen's Guild?' We used to meet in the folk centre and I think there were 200 members. There were quite a lot of young mums, and a crèche there for the babies, and it was great – adult company for one afternoon a week. Then it extended to two because they got me involved in the drama group. I was in several pantomimes, and the kids used to come along and sit and watch me, and giggle at mum on the stage.

Sue Lonsdale

Filton field days

Frances: Filton field days were wonderful. And the fair, twice a year. Gorgeous.
Margaret: Well, everybody used to join in.

Standing: Sue Lonsdale second left, Ann Churches far right.

... presents Pantomania 1984 – The Charlston.

Ken George, on the right, dressed for the fancy dress hockey on Filton Field Day in 1955.

Frances: All of Filton used to go to Filton field days.
Margaret: Yes, in fancy dresses. And the school, I remember doing the maypole dance there. Another year we did country dancing, and another year we did a shinty match. There was races and all sorts.
Frances: Fancy dress!
Margaret: Yeah, I went with Jill Phillips as the Bisto Kids, and you went as…
Frances: Mary Mary, and our Beth was Queen of Hearts.

Margaret Tarr and Frances Logan

BAC Sports Days on Southmead Road sports field

They were wonderful days, known far and wide, you know. They really were marvellous

days. There was so little recreation going on in those days that an occasion like a sports day was an Event.

Betty Beardmore

Boys will be boys

Margaret: BAC Sports Days down on the BAC sports ground.
Frances: They'd have the bands.
Margaret: And the beer tents, athletics and races and things like that down there. Every summer, in the early 1960s. There used to be big marquees up. My husband used to live just the other side. He'd go in, climb up the tents and slide down the roofs, until they got caught. They used to get under the veranda of the cricket pavilion and get long straws and poke them up ladies skirts. Wicked they were, wicked!

Margaret Tarr and Frances Logan

Filton folk centre

I am on the management of Filton Folk Centre and have been for thirty-two years. Years ago I was Entertainments Chairman and used to run dances every six weeks; the New Year's Eve Dance, the Valentines, a Spring Dance and a country dance in June. The Anniversary Fayre was in October because October was the month the building opened. We'd have a Guy Fawkes' Night and the children's party in December, and then go round again.

Ann Churches

Raising the money

The thing that started to pull people together again was the building of the Filton Folk Centre. They got money from the destruction of the memorial hall and that was the basic

Marquees on the Southmead Road BAC sports ground for the BAC Sports and Gala Day in June 1958. This was a major event, held in the 1950s. Attractions included cycle racing, athletics, cricket, archery, bowls, fancy dress and a horticultural show.

money. After that we had to raise the money ourselves. Well, everybody went 'vroomf'. We had 'beetle drives', and coffee mornings and coffee evenings, and dances, jumble sales and craft sales. You name it, we did it. So that was a heck of a day when the folk centre was opened by the Duchess of Beaufort.

Audrey Hawes

The Cabot Cinema (1950s)

You had a main film and a second film from seven o'clock till quarter past ten. It was a good showing; the prices were 1s 9d for the stalls, 2s 3d for the back of the stalls where they had double seats, upstairs in the balcony at the front was 2s 9d, and at the back of the balcony it was 2s 3d.

I can remember it always used to be blowing a gale. It's a very exposed corner, and you'd stand there, and it would be pouring down with rain, and you'd think 'What am I standing here for?' It was all out and around the corner, and then the commissionaire used to say 'I've got a single 1s 9d and a single at 2s 9d,' so if you were a pair you'd rush in and get those tickets, because when a film changed people came out,

so there was always a period of time when there were other seats available. The lights came on for the usherette to serve ice cream and cigarettes.

John Buckley

'Rock' at the Cabot

One occasion I remember going there and the film was *Blackboard Jungle*. That was the first time we heard 'Rock Around the Clock' by Bill Haley. I was there with my partner, and the manager came out onto the stage and threatened to throw anyone out if they got out of their seats and started dancing and really laid down the law for us before the film. This was something new, Rock and Roll music. 'Rock Around the Clock' was a step beyond as far as we were concerned.

Ken George

The Cabot Minors Club

Frances: Saturday morning pictures at the Cabot, wonderful, there'd be queues all the way along the road waiting to get in.

Maxine Latham created three pictures as part of the Filton Community History Millennium Project. This one covered the 1930s and 1940s.

Margaret: Sixpence a go.

Frances: And it was a swine when you got chewing gum or toffees in your hair if you were sat below.

Margaret: Stick in your hair if you were sat downstairs and they were upstairs.

Frances: And the film would break down wouldn't it? And the goodies and the baddies and the hissing and the booing.

Margaret: Stamping of feet, slapping of thighs, it makes me laugh! They'd ask if it was your birthday and you'd go up on the stage, and get sweets or something like a badge. And we'd all have to sing, it was lovely. It would be absolutely packed every Saturday.

Margaret Tarr and Frances Logan

Cliff-hangers

As a child, Saturday mornings were a great time. It used to cost me sixpence. I would go every Saturday morning, and there would be huge queues of children. We would have marvellous film shows and everybody in the area enjoyed that. *Flash Gordon* every week; it would finish with him in some predicament. There may have been a cowboy one as well and a serial. But the cinema was absolutely full.

Cliff Price

My first film

The first film that I was ever allowed to go out and see at the Cabot cinema was a Shirley

Temple thing. She sang 'On the good ship Lollipop', the first film I ever saw in the cinema. After that I used to go perhaps twice or three times a week.

Audrey Hawes

Will you take me in?

As a child I went to the Saturday matinées. I think it was threepence to go in. They had what you called a 'U' picture and an 'A' picture. If it was an 'A' you had to have another adult. My mother did a lot of knitting and she wasn't interested in the cinema. Nowadays you couldn't ask a perfect stranger to take you into the cinema. I never asked a man to take me in mind. The shop opposite used to sell broken ice creams and you'd have a big bag for a ha'penny. I used to buy gobstoppers, four for an old penny; they'd last ages and ages.

Phyllis Sutton

Pocket money at the polo field

If you go down Filton Hill there was a lane that went down to a polo field, now a rugby pitch. On Saturday afternoons when the polo players were coming, a lot of the younger children would go down and stand by the gate of the polo field, and as the cars came down we would open the gate. The window would go down on the car and pennies would be thrown out. My parents thought it was dreadful, begging.

Audrey Hawes

Street play

Two houses, old Mr T. lived in the first, and the second one was the village blacksmith. He was quite nice, but she was a little bit snooty. If ever we threw or kicked a ball and it went over their garden, you didn't get the ball back – we

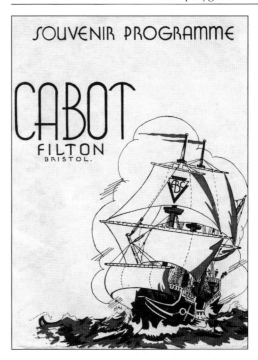

Souvenir programme celebrating the opening of the Cabot Cinema in 1935. This much-loved cinema continued to delight audiences until 1961. In 1962 it became a Fine Fare supermarket. It was demolished in the 1990s and a block of flats now occupies the site.

shouldn't have been playing there. She didn't like you playing. Sometimes we'd get a long piece of black cotton, we'd get over the church wall 'cos it was like level, and we'd tie it to the knocker. We used to knock and she'd come out to see who was at the door and of course it was no-one.

Pat Paice

Our playground

Mackie Avenue was our playground because it was flat. We used to come up here with whipping tops. We'd chalk the tops of the tops and when you whipped it, it spun round really fast. The patterns were lovely.

Sylvia Johnson

Sylvia Johnson, aged four, outside her home at 123 Mackie Road with her mother and brother in 1940.

Making toys out of firewood

My husband made a lot of toys then. He used to pinch all my wood for making a fire. He made a lot of toys, really a lot. Word went round the road, and you're making little ironing boards and a cot for dolls houses, and then he washed tins up to make a little dustpan and brush. There was a little boy across the road who come over with a mouse in his hand, asking 'Would you make a box for it?'

Mrs Breens

Severn Beach and the Blue Lagoon

[Severn Beach is about 10 miles from Filton]
I can remember coming out of BAC when I was about fifteen, and getting on my bike and cycling to Severn Beach and going into a swimming pool called the Blue Lagoon. That was open air, and if the temperature got to 63°F that was nice and warm.

Audrey Hawes

Home entertainment

Thirty-two shillings a week had to keep my father, mother, brother and myself, and they managed, we didn't go short of anything, but there were no luxuries. I can remember a radio that had to have a battery in it, an accumulator they called it. When it ran out, (you had two as a rule), you took one and had it charged up and used the other one. We used to gather round the radio and listen to things like *ITMA* (*It's That Man Again*) and *Round the Horn* and *Band Wagon*. The evening play was the thing on Saturday nights, and everybody had to be really quiet while we listened to the thrilling play on the radio.

Audrey Hawes

Hitch-hiking

Sometimes we'd go out to Severn Beach. We used to go there just to go in the open-air pool, and walk along the seafront. We used to like that. The times we walked there and hitched a lift – even as a child we used to hitch a lift.

Kristine White

Brown as a berry

I remember once I had a holiday and didn't go away. We spent it in the pool at the Blue Lagoon; about five cars used to go. We spent a whole week going backwards and forwards to Severn Beach, and I was as brown as a berry.

The Passage Road end of Severn Beach in the 1920s. The Blue Lagoon was behind the sea wall.

When I went into the dining room on Monday, one of the Board of Directors of BAC turned to me and said 'You didn't get that tan here.' I said 'I did, in the Blue Lagoon,' he looked as much as to say 'where's that'?

Thelma Ryczko

Going by train

Many the time's me and a mate went down to Severn Beach on the train to the Blue Lagoon. It was only a little village, and Severn Beach as I remember it, has gone.

Phyllis Sutton

Severn Beach fun

I can remember the old fairground they had down there, the old few shops, a few bungalows dotted around, the little kiddies railway, the house of a miniature railway and things to keep people happy. It was lovely, and the cost was what I call coppers.

Phyllis Sutton

Holidays

We had to lug cases and buckets and spades and you name it up Filton Hill, and get on a tram to go into Bristol. My father used to lug the cases from the Tramway Centre to Temple Meads Station. We looked forward to it from the day we left the previous year because that was special. Not many children had holidays like that in those days. We could only do it because my father was employed by Great Western Railway.

Audrey Hawes

Sleeping out

In the summer holidays we used to get sacks, split them open, and with brush handles, build a sack tent. We'd put a ground sheet down and sleep out all night. Mother used to come down in the mornings to see we were all right. When we wanted something for dinner, there was an allotment just there, so we'd pull up a couple of potatoes, and put them on the coke fire. When they were done, we used to

Phillip Shield in 1911.

take off the black and eat them. We used to go blackberrying and go down and watch the trains.

I used to go down to Duchesses Lake in Stapleton and turn up left next to the river, to Snuff Mills. When we were kids, Mother used to say 'Don't get in the water,' and that was the first thing we did, only paddling!

Phillip Shield

A day out

I can remember going as a child over to Duchesses, to Snuff Mills, and our mum used to give us two jam sandwiches, and maybe if we were lucky we'd get a penny off of her and we'd go over to Snuff Mills. Where the MOD is now, that was fields and a public walkway, and we used to go across there and walk through this farmer's field. We used to be petrified because he had black Labrador dogs, and every time we walked on that path his dogs would come out after us and we used to stand there petrified. The dogs used to bark and bark, and he used to have to call them back. Then we went through the woods and down over the Duchesses, and you weren't allowed to stop because it was private land. There was a little shop down in the corner and we used to go in there and buy a penny lollipop, dome lollipop, like a dome, and that was our treat.

Kristine White

A Long walk

A big treat during the summer holidays was to get the bus with mum to Eastville Park by where the Rovers ground used to be, walk through Eastville Park and Snuff Mills, ending up at Duchesses Ponds at Stapleton by that big old house – the Dower House. Then we used to walk through to Filton across the fields and over the railway bridge which is now the cycle path into Kipling Road, and then we used to get the bus home along Filton Avenue. It was a real treat.

Geoff Lonsdale

St Peter's church socials and Sunday school

Any sort of entertainment revolved around the church. We used to have church socials, church outings, but you were only allowed to go on the outings if you attended Sunday school regularly and you were given marks for attendance. In the summer you'd go on a charabanc to Weston-super-Mare, which was absolutely fabulous. All dressed up in our best and off to go; sun, wind, rain anything, it didn't matter. We were going to Weston-super-Mare!

Audrey Hawes

Seaside visits

I went to Filton church to the Sunday school, three times a day – I loved it. We went on outings, mainly to Weston and Portishead. Little sorts of what we called charabancs, we'd take our swimming or paddling gear. It was a lovely village.

Phyllis Sutton

Pubs

Pat: There was the... oh God, The Galleon. Now, what was it?
Hilda: The Beeches.
Pat: Before the Beeches it was the Gaynor's, the Gaynor's had it and they were…
Hilda: Quakers.
Pat: They had it converted into a club, so that was a spot we used to go.
Hilda: They'd have a piano, and one man in particular, he was a good entertainer.
Pat: And the Shoe and the Plough. Well, then the George VI came on the scene, didn't it?

The Dower House, part of the Beaufort Estate, on the hill above Duchesses pond on the footpath from Filton to Snuff Mills.

Filton Methodist Church sunday school outing to Clevedon in the 1950s.

Hilda: We never went to the Anchor much. We never sort of liked that pub all that much for some unknown reason. We used to use the Shoe because mum was up there serving, but we'd use the Plough because there was so much going on there with old Jim Peters.

Hilda Saunders and Pat Paice

Different times

The Fellowship was in Bristol, and The Bulldog was in Filton, and the licensing laws were different. The Fellowship closed at ten; in Filton the pubs closed at half past ten. So the bus used to stop outside The Fellowship at ten o'clock, and half the bar would pile on and come down for another half-hour's drinking – back in the 1950s and '60s or later.

Ken George

The Aces Club

The Aces Club was at the Bristol Siddeley Technical College at the foot of Filton Hill. They served coffee only. I think they wanted to

keep the apprentices on the straight and narrow. It was just somewhere to go. We'd usually end up at the Anchor, or somewhere like that.

Tim Bowly

Club activities

I got married in 1962 to a girl from Southmead. She worked at BAC and we met at the marvellous Apprentice Association (BAC Aces). Many of the people that lived in the area and worked at BAC were welcome at the Aces. It kept many young people off the streets. There were many activities. I became chairman of the ballroom dancing club. Every Friday evening we carried the equipment across to Filton Hill School, and used their hall for the ballroom dancing club. Many other clubs were organised by the company.

Cliff Price

Street parties

Well, it was just the basic street party, with tables laid out and everything, and we had clowns and jesters and people doing all sorts of tricks. A pony and trap ride – he managed to give everyone a lift up the road and back again. But of course the money was restricted, so we couldn't hope for too much excitement. The mothers made all the cakes, buns and jellies.

Rodney Hewett

Community Spirit

In 1953, which was Coronation year, we had a street party for children in this road, and it was wet, and we asked for permission and had it up at the pavilion. The mothers brought all the food. I think people came together more in those days, with the children and the war, and they would all join in, masses of them.

Mrs R.

Playing football

I used to go to the Cabot Cinema, ABC Minors on a Saturday morning, and for sport I played football. Whenever I could find a ball, I played football in the streets, and in the field at the back of the house.

Rodney Hewett

Playing in the fields

Mrs G.: We used to get shouted at if anyone saw us in the fields. We used to go in and collect the chrysalises on the grasses. If anyone saw you they would shout at you.
Mr G.: If the farmer saw you first.
Mrs G.: So many rules. They used to cut the hay and gather it up. We used to play in it when it was cut and dry. You could build a house, you can imagine.

Mackie Road street party with pony cart rides. Rodney Hewett is the fair-haired boy in the light-coloured shirt standing on the right edge of the picture.

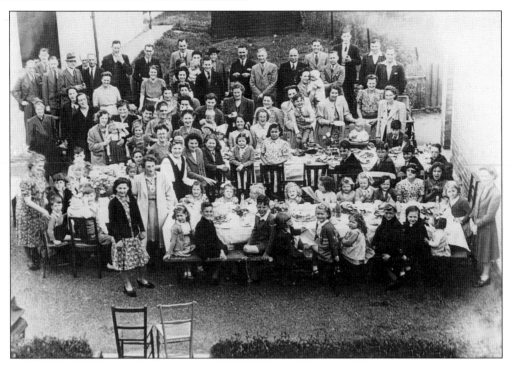

A Mackie Road street party.

They didn't mind you playing in it so much then, but not running in it before it was cut.

Mr and Mrs G.

Lads at play

I'd go to this field up here and there'd be twenty cricket matches going on, with perhaps only half a dozen lads, a coat or a few sticks stuck in the ground, a bat and a few balls, going on all over the field. Never see it now, and the kids say that they haven't got anything to do. That is one of the big differences you know; they haven't learnt how to amuse themselves with a bat!

Ken George

6 Filton at War

As the location of the largest aviation complex in the world, Filton came in for special attention from the enemy. In September 1940 there were two daylight raids, in which several shelters on the airfield and local houses received direct hits. We hear stories of the raids and of everyday life during this period of shortages and make do and mend.

War is declared

On the morning of Sunday 3 September 1939, I hadn't gone to church. Sometimes I used to have to go to church three times on a Sunday – the eleven o'clock service, Sunday school in the afternoon and then evensong. On this particular morning, everybody was worrying about what the announcement was going to be on the radio. I was stood with my mother at the kitchen table and we were slicing runner beans – I can remember that as if it was yesterday – and we had the radio on. It suddenly came over the radio that there had been no reply from Germany to say that they would get out of Poland, and therefore this country was at war with Germany. I can remember my mother crying and saying to her 'Why are you crying mummy? Daddy won't have to go, he's too old.'

Audrey Hawes

Recruiting ARP volunteers in the vestibule of the Cabot Cinema in 1939.

Preparations

The ARP, (Air Raid Precautions) people came round and fitted us up with gas masks. We all had to have identity cards, and they come round asking did we want an Anderson shelter in the garden?

In the little block of houses that we were in they all said 'Oh no we shan't need anything like that,' but my father said 'We will have one, we might need it.' They came along, dug this big hole in the garden, and fitted us up with this Anderson shelter. Father put earth all over the top of it, and it just sat there, and as I say, it was the only one in that block of houses. Then one night the sirens went! We all came downstairs and gathered in what we used to call the middle room. All of a sudden there was this loud whistle – 'fsswee' – and I didn't know what it was, but my father did because he'd been in the First World War. He said 'My God! He's bombing!' and one bomb dropped somewhere near the golf links. So as soon as the thud came and the bang, my dad said 'Right, we'd better get out to the shelter,' having never used the wretched thing before. When we got out in the garden to the shelter, we couldn't get in because all the neighbours were in there! They'd crowded into the shelter so we had to go back in and hide under the stairs.

There was a big car park down at the back of the house where we lived. We had loads of fun laughing at them all as they came in and put wire netting all over this big car park, daubed it with some sort of solution and threw feathers at it. These feathers stuck to the solution, and then of course, they came along with paint and they camouflaged it. I suppose it was meant to look like a forest or something, but I mean there were feathers everywhere, just everywhere you looked there was feathers drifting about! We all thought that was a huge joke.

Audrey Hawes

Evacuated

I was evacuated at Donyatt in Somerset, just north of Chard, on a farm.

One frightening experience I had there was I was on my way to school, which was about a mile-and-a-half to two miles away, and I had to walk. There was a railway bridge, and under the railway bridge came three tanks, and I thought we'd been invaded. I went screaming back up the road to the farm. It was actually only the manoeuvres for the British tanks. They kept me at home all day for that; I was a bit upset!

Rodney Hewett

The daylight raid – 25 September 1940

In my opinion the air-raid shelters had been built a bit too close together, I guess because they had to get a lot of them in. But the bomb that got me landed right between two shelters, and just caved them in on both sides. Normally I would have been sitting right in the middle, where everybody was killed, but I had a detective novel Mum didn't like. I was sixteen at the time, and used to take it to read when we went down the shelters, and I had to sit by the door to read which saved my life. In the centre where the light was they were all killed. The whole shelter was collapsed in, and that's where my friends were and where I would have been sitting if it hadn't been for that trashy book. We could hear the bombers coming. Each shelter had its own warden; he was standing outside looking up, and the last thing I remember he jumped inside saying 'Get down quick!' He saw a stick of bombs coming, and then there was a huge bang. There wasn't time to hear any whistle, just a big bang. I did what my father had told me to do; because I was young I could do it. I put my head down between my knees, covered

Wartime air-raid shelters alongside the A38 beside Filton Airfield, taken in 1996.

The air-raid shelter on the internal road between the airfield and Golf Course Lane, taken in 2002.

the back of my head with my hands; that saved my life. Had I been sitting upright I would have been dead like a lot of the other guys, because the concrete was like shrapnel, it just cut them down. I was lucky. I just got injuries to the back of my arms and my head, and got hit in the head a couple of times. There was a dead man right across my lap. I was only sixteen – I'd never seen a dead man before. He was covered in blood. I pushed him away. I heard this big man come to the entrance of the door which was crumbling in, a great big guy. He came in and picked me up like a feather, and carried me off to the first aid post. When I recuperated at that first aid post, they said 'Well just wait here a minute, we'll get transport for you,' and a great big black Rolls-Royce drove up to that post and picked me up

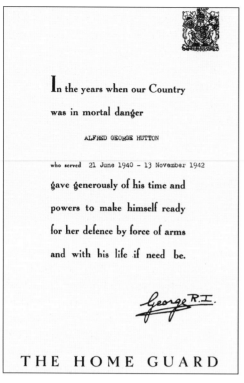

In the years when our Country
was in mortal danger

ALFRED GEORGE HUTTON

who served   21 June 1940 – 13 November 1942

gave generously of his time and
powers to make himself ready
for her defence by force of arms
and with his life if need be.

George R.I.

THE HOME GUARD

John Hutton's Home Guard certificate, signed by King George VI.

and took me home. That was really something. I was very lucky – I just had a nasty bang on the head. I went home and my house was sitting there, the roof and the windows blown in, but everybody was glad to see me!

Roy Mockridge

The Wednesday raids

Bert joined the Home Guard at BAC, and he was up on Purdown for quite a while on the big gun that was up there. We were here on the Wednesday raids in Filton.

I think the worst was waiting for the men to come home. Some would come down, and their coats would be ragged, like. Bert came home, it must have been teatime, and he said

'Don't worry if there's noises tonight, it will be unexploded bombs going off.' He had to go back on Home Guard out at the 'drome that night, which wasn't very pleasant for us.

Mrs R.

Looking for Roy

My father worked at Rodney, but he wasn't at work that day. He had a day off and had gone down to the Odeon in Bristol with his Mum. Coming back on the bus to Filton you can imagine what their thoughts were, on seeing all the ambulances and fire engines; they thought they would never see us again. But we were just very, very lucky. I lost several good friends, including the lodger who was staying with us. He was in the centre and I would have been sat right next to him if it hadn't been for that book. So the book saved my life. Poor old Dad, they put the bodies in Filton church, and he had to go around and try to find me. That wasn't very nice.

Roy Mockridge

Alone in a shelter

We got to Victoria Park at about ten o'clock, and the sirens went. They used to play 'Marching through Georgia', and that was the BAC's warning to get to shelter. My mother said to me 'You go to the shelter and we'll come out and join you later on.' So all of a sudden, I think it was ninety-seven aircraft came over, and dropped eighty-odd tonnes of bombs, just like that 'whoosh'! At school we'd been told air-raid drill, so I said to Dennis, my cousin 'Put your fingers in your ears, shut your eyes like that, open your mouth and sit on the floor.' It was all over so quickly that it was unbelievable. My father had put earth over the shelter and it was just a mass of colour with nasturtiums. When I got up to get hold of this corrugated door to pull it in the gap, I was only eleven and I didn't know anymore. The door went; it was sort of blown right out of my hands. I got down on the floor with my cousin, and there we stayed, shaking from head to foot, scared out of our wits.

When everything went quiet there was this terrible smell of burning and cordite and everything else. We just sat, didn't speak, didn't move and then a nurse eventually came along and looked in the shelter and saw us and said 'Where are your parents?' I said 'Well, my mother's in that house over there with his mother, I expect they'll be in the cupboard under the stairs,' because that was where everybody went. So she said 'Well you stay where you are and I'll go and find them.' Off she went, and she did find them. The jam jars and pots of jam had shattered, and they'd come down on top of them. They were all covered with jam and porridge oats and everything under the sun. My mother was not injured but sort of paralysed with fear, I think.

When we came out of that shelter, there wasn't a scrap of earth. It was as naked as the day it was put in; everything had been blown off, and there were two big shrapnel holes in the corrugated iron. Shrapnel had come in through in two places and missed us. Neither of us was touched.

Audrey Hawes

Air raids in Filton

I can remember when the soldiers marched up Filton Hill, past the airfield, when there was German planes overhead, and they swooped down and machine-gunned the lot. Some of the lorries that had soldiers in, and they machine-gunned them. The German planes were really knocking hell out of Filton airfield. I can remember the old Spitfires going up and dogfights over the airfield. Mum, Jean and I were going visiting somebody at Patchway, and while walking down past the

Phyllis Sutton with her granddaughter Samantha in 1989.

airfield the sirens went. Our mum said 'God, we'd better run like mad now to get to Coniston Road.' The policeman came outside of the gate, looked at my mother and said 'You silly buggers! What are you doing?' He said 'Come on in, get in this shelter.'

Another laughable thing was when they used to come over and the sirens did go, mum didn't always go down in the shelter. This particular day, it was a daytime raid, and she was out shaking her mats. The Spitfires and the German planes were coming over. Our mum was out there and she was waving her brush at them; 'Go on, give them what for!' And they did, mind. It was a wonderful sight to see, but it was a frightening sight to see as well.

Phyllis Sutton

Fuelling up for action

When an air raid occurred, two things happened. First of all, the lorries came down from the Works to fill up with petrol, and then they dispersed so that they weren't in the depot. Second thing that happened was that the local builders turned up to get their AFS engine 'cos the Auxiliary Fire Service were really volunteers, builders and people like that, very much like the lifeboat service today. People arrived from all over, got the fire engine out, put on the uniform, steel helmet and waited. Communication was the telephone, there wasn't walkie-talkie or anything like that and we had a telephone, incidentally one of the earliest telephones 'cos the number was Filton 49.

John Buckley

Surviving the bombing raids

I remember my Gran. She was a tiny little lady, and she used to have this tiny little case with all her treasures in it, you know, her insurance policy and all that sort of thing, and she used to trot down to the air-raid shelter and stay there.

Sylvia Johnson

Memories of wartime air raids

We used to have candles in a little lantern; you could open the door and light the candle and shut the glass door for use when the air raids were taking place. There was a daylight raid on 25 September 1940. I was in the garden and I could see aeroplanes in the sky circling about, travelling from east to west. They dropped bombs. Houses in Station Road got damaged, and in Mackie Road.

It was Good Friday in 1941, about midnight. An air-raid warning had been sounded for some time and we hadn't even bothered to go to the shelter that night. Three bombs were dropped, the first of which exploded. The third one sounded very noisy and close. I thought it was coming down our chimney, but it landed just next door. Two houses were completely demolished, and the two either side were knocked down soon afterwards. We walked out soon after midnight; put a coat on over our pyjamas. We didn't stop at the first air-raid shelter; we went on to a brick built service shelter at the top of Wades Road. We were there a few minutes. We then went up to an air-raid shelter at No. 2 Conygre Road, and then from there we went to another air-raid shelter between the laundry house and the laundry. After a while, I think we left that one and went to an air-raid shelter between the parish hall and the laundry, and eventually we put up for the night at the top of Southmead Road in one of those houses.

John Hutton

The Good Friday raid

On the Good Friday, I was out the front, and there was a plane in the searchlights and I could actually see the bombs leave the plane. The next thing you knew I could hear this whistling, so I dived into the passageway. There was this horrific bang and they'd hit a house up on Station Road, and it killed a family, all but one. They thought there was an unexploded bomb in the house next door to us, so we had to get out. We had to go to Shield Road School, so we were walking with our shoes and our best clothes in our hands. We got to the top of Wades Road and some ARP men there said 'Where do you reckon you lot are going? Oh no you don't,' he said, so we had to turn around and come back, and we didn't know where to go. The woman who had the Horseshoe, she took us in, but she didn't give us a drink, we had nothing, and we sat there all night, on our chairs, waiting for day to come. That was a night, terrible.

Hilda Saunders

Civil Defence volunteers practise rescue techniques on Conygre House in the 1940s.

A low-flying plane

I can remember being down the shelters in the war, you know, it was quite horrific out there. We didn't have all that much bombing, but what we did have was quite terrible. I was running round to a neighbour, and I can remember seeing a German aeroplane coming across quite low. I could see the cross on the wings. I think that was a reconnaissance plane for the raids.

Betty Beardmore

After the bombing

To recuperate, they sent me over to my Auntie's house, which was in Ashton. The following day she called me out into the yard, and said 'Look, they're coming again.' There was a big dogfight going on, but this time the Spitfires were there to meet them. One of them came tumbling down in flames, so I felt pretty good about that.

When I tried to go back to work, there weren't many left alive. That tool room shelter sat fifty people. I think there was just four or five who got out.

Roy Mockridge

Orange juice and cod liver oil

We used to walk down to Conygre House to get orange juice for the children and some cod liver oil. Before the Church View shops there was two cottages and they sold mint.

Mrs Breens

Making a new home

When we got this house at the bottom of Northville we needed to furnish it somehow. Nobody could buy furniture, or carpets or curtains or mattresses. They just weren't about, so it was hilarious really. They got a big truck, a big wagon, brought it out to the house and piled into this truck whatever they could find that was useable. I was coming home from school up Midland Road and there was this big truck coming down the road with a flag, a Union Jack fluttering on the top of it, and my mother sat in the middle with all this junk on the back of this truck.

Audrey Hawes

Bristol is bombed (c. 1940)

During the war, the old school room was taken over as a YMCA for the troops, and I used to work over there. I'd been on duty in the afternoon, and I just popped over home. I was going back over to do an evening when our eldest brother said to me 'Where do you think you're going?' and I said 'I'm going back over the YM.' 'Oh no you're not,' he said, 'you get back in there under the stairs,' and I said 'why?' and he said 'look at that,' and you could see all the red glow where they'd had a raid on Bristol. God knows what it was like down there, but it looked terrible from where we were.

Hilda Saunders

Beer for the BAC workers, and cider for the strangers

During the war, old Jim Peters at the Plough used to have two deliveries a week 'cos of the ammunitions they were building at the Works, and if the beer ran out old Jim used to serve all the beer in cider mugs to the locals. Any stranger come in it was cider only. All the blimmin' Yanks, they used to come out and get this cider: 'let's have some of the Apple Jack, man.'

Sid Chilcott

We never went short

You could go into the canteens at the BAC and buy a cheese roll that had as much cheese on it as a person's ration for the whole week. Blokes used to go in there and buy them, and throw the roll away and take the cheese home for the family.

I lived on a chicken farm so I never remember being short of eggs, and my mother used to work on the farm sorting potatoes, so I never remember being short of potatoes.

Ken George

Southmead Garage

The petrol sold in wartime was 'pool petrol'. People coming along to buy petrol had to have coupons, and you bought one coupon for one. You carried a bit of paper, an order, to give you authority to travel on the road. After 1944-'45, my mother used to drive the car, and she used to say 'right Cyril, give me an order to go to town to collect spare parts,' which was an excuse for her to go to town to collect shopping and have tea somewhere.

John Buckley

Under the counter

I had to go up Braemar Avenue to register to get our rations, and there was Pearks and Home Colonial, but I chose Pearks because for me they were London shops.

There was a butcher's shop that's still there. I knew granddad Millhouse, his son Roy, and his grandsons are there now. My youngest daughter was fond of meat, so the granddad found me some meat under the counter, which was wrong really, but then the rations…

Mrs Breens

Make do and mend

New clothes had become something of the past, because you had to have coupons, and you could have very little in the way of clothing in the teenage years. This is why we really suffered. Because you couldn't buy much, it was make do and mend nearly all the time. You spent the odd coupon or two of course, but when you think about it, what's more important – a warm pair of socks or stockings and some underclothes, or something fancy on top?

Ms W.

Digging for Victory

Mr Breens: I know I used to have an allotment down the other side of our way.
Mrs Breens: He dug for victory too, planted potatoes. Well, there's a picture, you're in it aren't you? On that book *Dig For Victory*, planting potatoes and digging potatoes. Although they weren't fighting you know like going to Germany.
Mr Breens: We dug for victory.

Mr and Mrs Breens

The Filton British Restaurant

On the Gloucester Road there was a British Restaurant. A lot of it was bombed. It was just along past there that we had our hall, Filton Hall, before this new one, Filton Folk Centre.

Mrs R.

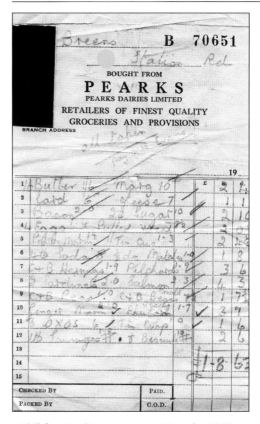

A bill from Peark's grocery store in November 1949.

Rationing

There was a place called a British Restaurant where you could go and have a meal without coupons, a cheap nourishing meal that wasn't rationed. You couldn't get anything; sugar, butter, tea, sweets, clothing, bread, coal, petrol, everything was rationed; so you could have a certain amount but no more. So the British Restaurant was a godsend, we could go and have a meal. It's now Sinclair House, elderly people's sheltered accommodation.

Audrey Hawes

Mr and Mrs Breens in their garden in 1996.

Pooling resources

Everybody was so pleased to have so little then that life was very different. Any excuse for a party, and we used to save up our little bits of cooking fat and butter and stuff like that to make a few cakes maybe, and my mother used to mix her butter ration with margarine and a little bit of top of the milk to make it go further, and make sandwiches. We'd get together and have a singsong around the piano, and thoroughly enjoy ourselves until the sirens went. Then it was all put a stop to, and you had to get down to the shelter just as you were. On Sunday mornings I used to get up and go over to the next-door neighbour, and she'd give me her fat and bits and pieces, and pool it with my mother's, and I used to come back in, put the two lots of ingredients together so that we had enough and make fruit pies. And they'd have one fruit pie and we'd have a fruit pie. You couldn't do it alone because the quantity wasn't big enough to make anything worthwhile, but if you pooled things you could do it.

Audrey Hawes

Americans in Filton

I remember the Americans. They used to come along to what was then the Cabot Cinema. My father was a sergeant in the special police. It was one of his jobs to see them out quietly at night, and he used to stand in the shop doorway until all the fighting and everything else was over after they came out of the cinema, and then they used to wander along to the station and say 'All quiet Sir' to the inspector, which it was by then!

Ms W.

American riches

They had things we'd never seen. They used to have huge parties up at Horfield Barracks. The girls were invited because they would have dances. We used to vie with each other to get an invitation to these parties, because they had butter and sugar, and chewing gum and nylons, Spam and ham; they had so much foodstuff that we hadn't seen for years that the Americans' parties were legendary. The boys didn't like their girls going out with the Americans. We all had American boyfriends, but they all went home and we stayed here. I suppose there were a few that got themselves into trouble, the ones I knew were just genuine away from home lads. The dances were fabulous – the big band sound, Glen Miller, that sort of band sound.

Audrey Hawes

Avoiding the raids

Pat: The family next door, he was a lorry driver. Sometimes he would bring the lorry home, and if we thought there was going to be a bad raid we'd all of us get on the back of the lorry and go out in the country until it was all over, out sort of Stoke Gifford way.

Hilda: I always remember one night we were

The Duchess of Beaufort has lunch after opening the Filton British Restaurant in February 1942. Mr A.W. Britton is next to the Duchess on the right.

stopped in this sort of lane, and all of a sudden, the other side of the hedge was an 'ack–ack', and it opened up and frightened the life out of us.

Hilda Saunders and Pat Paice

A clever move?

The whole war bound society together more than it has ever been before or since, because we were all going through it. We were being bombed every flipping night for quite a while. During the big blitz, we had to move twice because we had no roof over our heads. My Dad got a clever idea, and took a holidaymakers' cabin down at Portishead and got away from the blitz. On the second night we were there 'Jerry' came over, dropping sea mines by parachute, and one of them drifted over and hit the beach about a quarter of a mile away, and that cabin went about six feet off the floor!

Roy Mockridge

Lulsgate decoy

During the war we went from here to Lulsgate because of the bombing, which was a mistake because they built the large decoy on the ground that is now the airport, and we had bombs down the side of the house. Everybody in the village used to get into and onto all the cars that were available, and go down to Cheddar Gorge at night when they heard the planes coming over, dogs, cats and everything.

Ms W.

A narrow escape

I was in the house with Mother, when the siren went. I put my little tin helmet on and dashed to the air-raid shelter. Mum was busy turning off the water and the gas as you usually do, and I was standing at the door of the air raid shelter. I heard this big bomber coming over, a big black thing, and it was

Cliff Price, aged three, with his sister Evelyn outside their Anderson shelter.

remember one of them coming here was the Friday morning raid after the Wednesday one.

The sirens went, and we ran down to the Anderson shelter – they put all those in for us; every house had one. We heard a rustling, and it was one of these airmen, and he dashed in and got in our shelter with us.

Mrs R.

Holiday Inn

The field behind our house in Mackie Avenue used to have a barrage balloon, and it came down and smashed Dad's beans and his cabbages. All the RAF blokes were there, scrambling over the garden and flattening all his vegetables for the following year! At the top of the field was an American company – I don't know what they actually did. They had a big hut there and a big gun, a Bofors, and they called the hut the Holiday Inn, from the film. The Yanks gave me some shoulder insignias to stick on my jersey and things like that. They were there in about 1944 when I was eleven or twelve. They used to give us comics – Batman, Superman and Dan Dare.

Rodney Hewett

Guns on Elm Park

The field behind was a cricket ground, but during the war it had gun emplacements, so you had areas of about fifteen foot square concrete with a ring of bolts in the centre for bolting guns down. There must have been about half a dozen of those. When I was young there was a concrete tower in the field with a gun on top of that, and some searchlights, and a shed for housing the people that ran them.

Ken George

very, very low. Mum ran up the garden path, and the thing was so close she ran back down to the house again, and I was shouting 'come on Mum, come on now,' but she ran back down to the neighbour's house. The machine gun was going off all the time. I could see her hiding, pressed against the wall, and he actually fired a few shots at her and hit the wall above her head, and she was covered in dust from the machine gun bullets.

Rodney Hewett

Barrage balloons

Jane was the balloon, and they had written a big 'Jane'. We got to know them a bit because they would cut across to go to the shops, which was a field at the back where the allotments are. The only time I can

Fools rush in!

The Germans dropped land mines on Olveston village. My cousin, some of their mates and some of the older youths started defusing the mines. When the local bobby got wind of this, he got onto the army and the bomb disposal squad. When they came in they found several of them had been defused by youths that had never been in the army!

Phyllis Sutton

Revenge!

I did get my own back. A few months later I was on the anti-aircraft guns. I was in the Home Guard at sixteen, firing anti-aircraft rockets. There was 150 guns in that field, and on each one two rockets. That was 300 rockets going up at the planes, all in one 'swoosh'. At least if we didn't hit any of them at least we scared them to death. The rocket was six feet tall, and about eight inches around. You picked them up and slid them on the two shafts. You had headphones and you listened for your orders; you set the horizontal and the vertical and waited for the order to fire, and we all fired at the same time so you had 150 guns shooting 300 rockets. That was really something to see. And on the night of the Baedeker raids on all the cathedral towns in England, they went for Bath, and we got one that night. That was my moment of revenge. Anyway, I survived the flipping lot. They tried hard to get me but they didn't quite make it.

Roy Mockridge

Roy Mockridge on a fleeting visit to Filton from his home in California, USA, in August 2002.

7 Working at BAC

Sir George White's British and Colonial Aeroplane Company flew its first Boxkite in 1910. This family industry went from strength to strength, becoming Bristol Aeroplane Company (BAC), then British Aircraft Corporation (BAC) and then British Aerospace. Now named Airbus UK, this massive concern completely overwhelmed the quiet hilltop village, absorbing several farmhouses. The engine division, later Bristol Siddeley, was taken over by Rolls-Royce. About 40,000 people worked at the factory during the war.

Gardener

Our granddad was one of the first employees at the BAC. He did all the gardens. Down Filton Hill there was a row of cherry trees all the way down, and he planted all those. They used to look lovely every spring.

Frances Logan

Sunday lunch

You used to be able to get into BAC easily when I was small, 'cos I used to take Dad's cooked dinner in on a Sunday when he used to work over. Mum cooked his dinner and put it in a basket, and I used to go up. The man on the gate knew me and he'd say 'You know where to go.' I used to go in and wander all round by the apple trees, and into the tinsmith's shop.

Mrs G.

Timekeeping

Working at BAC was quite hard going, because you started at 8.30 a.m. and you had a card, a clock card, and you went in and you had to push it down in the machine and press. It went 'ding', and recorded the time you came in, so if you were late it was noted. You weren't allowed to be late. We'd break for an hour for lunch, 12.30-1.30 p.m., and then we'd work through to 5.30 p.m. And on Saturdays we used to work 8.30 p.m. to 12.30 p.m., so that was a five-and a-half day week. And at holiday times you had Christmas Day and Boxing Day, and nothing else. You had one week's holiday a year.

Audrey Hawes

Being late for work

They were very strict about timekeeping. You were hauled over the coals if you were a few minutes late, and this was wartime and I was fourteen. I can remember standing in tears in front of Mr A.'s desk while he said 'Miss Pearce, you were...' well, it was only a matter of minutes late, in a whole week, and I was stood there in tears, saying 'But Mr A., the bus was late.' He said to me 'Well, you must catch an earlier bus.' He said 'I'm never late,' and he wasn't. We used to run like mad at Shield's clock to clock in on time, because you knew you would be 'for it'.

Betty Beardmore

The clock on Samuel Shield's Laundry was a timely check for BAC workers.

Staff and workers

Being a family company there was a strict hierarchy. There were the workers, and there was the staff. Staff were paid sick pay. If they got married they were given a week's leave with pay. They had a different canteen; on staff clock cards they had 'Mr J. Bloggs'. On the Works cards, you had 'Bloggs, J'. They even got different cough mixture if they went to the ambulance room. There was class distinction right through. It used to work in opposite ways 'cos when you went to the canteen, the same serving area served the staff on the other side, and they had to pay more for their food than we did.

You started at half past seven. If you hadn't arrived by eight o'clock the clock cards were removed from the racks, and you couldn't start until the start of the next shift at one o'clock – you lost half a day's pay. But this was much better than Hills Dockyard in Bristol, where you got three minutes. At three minutes past half past seven, the gates closed and you couldn't start again until the afternoon shift.

Mike Jones

Fairlawn Avenue

I worked in Fairlawn Avenue, which is no longer there. It was inside the BAC premises, but they were privately owned houses, and people lived in them. As they became empty they were turned into offices.

Audrey Hawes

Lucky to get a job

I was lucky in those days (1930s) to get a job, mind you. I started off as a shop boy, a sort of errand boy some might say, and I had to get through a crowd of blokes to get to the

Fairlawn Avenue. The row of houses on the bottom right side of the picture was built in 1908 for the workers at the new tramways garage to rent. The avenue was a turning off Homestead Road and part of the village of Filton until the 1930s, when wartime security measures closed the site. The houses were later used as offices, and demolished in the 1990s. The new Filton House and Shield Laundry are to the top of the picture.

blimmin' employment place; full of blokes outside in the yard, and we were all stood outside waiting.

Sid Chilcott

Early computers (c. 1960s)

Frances: I worked up at Bristol Aeroplane Company for a while, as an IBM (International Business Machines) operator, little punchcard machines, computers. With a punch pool of about sixty of us, I was doing all the wages, bonuses and various other things. We all got on really well. We had some good times. We collected up some money, so we bought all the drink in for the Christmas party, and the apprentices used to come over and have a few drinks. This one Christmas, everybody got absolutely legless, and two of the girls got taken home in the director's car.

I was on £9 a week; that was really good at the time.

Margaret: Yeah it was good money. When I started working at Lewis' in 1957 I was on good money at £3 and 15 shillings a week.

Frances Logan and Margaret Tarr

Design work at Rolls-Royce

I designed a lot of forging blades. All the blades in the engine were made from precision forgings, and it was quite a specialist job designing them. They closed the blade forge down just after I stopped working there.

I was sixteen years on the drawing board, and twenty-five years on production control engineering. I was lucky in that I always had a job that was interesting, and a job that didn't always tie me to a desk. When I was on the blade forging, I'd have to go and liaise with design, 'cos we were already designing the 'dies' before the finished drawing was complete. So we had to go and find out what they were going to draw 'cos it takes a long time to make a 'die'. Your time scale was nine months; if you could cut a month off it then all's well.

I was a Union representative at the office for a long time. They called it Corresponding Member, but it was like a shop steward in the office. There was the Association of Engineering and Shipbuilding Draughtsmen, and it was very, very closed, in that you had to work on the drawing board or be a planning engineer to be a member. This tended to make you a little bit more elite. Then the unions wanted more power, more people. They extended it to technicians, and eventually it was an all encompassing union; much stronger as I said because of more members, but a lot weaker, I think, in that they never had the quality.

We had a big strike whilst I was there in 1963. We were out for six weeks. The union paid us full take-home pay, and I was on the strike organisation involved with the paying of half of them that worked this side of Gypsy Patch. There were a thousand people on strike, and they were getting something like £20 a week average, and I had 500 people's money under my bed. Thieves could have got away with £10,000! This house in 1961 cost £2,000.

I spent the majority of my life working on the Pegasus, starting when I finished my apprenticeship, right through to the end of my working life. At the end I was Senior Project Engineer over about six guys who were all working on an engine each. My engine was Pegasus.

Ken George

Globetrotting

Margaret: My father, Frank Booth, was an engineer, and a Chief Inspector when he retired. He worked on the Brabazon, Britannia and Concorde.

Frances: Mr Spiller, he went to Karachi and our dad went with him. An aircraft crashed right up in the hills, and they had to go out with him and mend it. He was away seven months. He went all round the country working on Bloodhound missiles.

Frances Logan and Margaret Tarr

Working away

When Concorde went into service, the engineers in charge of the project decided that the very first engine on a Concorde aircraft that completed 800 cycles, (a cycle is a take-off to landing and would equate to about 2,000 hours), the first engine to meet that milestone would be stripped, and given an in-depth inspection right the way through all the major rotating components. As it happened, the first engine to

Ken George, twenty years old in 1955.

do that came off a French Concorde, and the French were having their Concorde engines overhauled in Madrid. Two people were chosen to go down to Madrid to do the inspection on this Concorde engine, and I was one of the two. Initially we were there for three weeks, and then, because not all the components were available, we had to come back. I went back about four or five times for shorter periods.

I travelled around in this country as well on different projects. When the Harrier was flying first I went up to Dunsford a couple of times to do checks. I've been to Woodford at Manchester where the Vulcans were built, working on the Olympus engines. Concorde engines were undergoing tests at Pyestock at the National Gas Turbine Establishment, so I've been up there a few times. It went with the job, you travelled around.

Phil Kirley

Frances Logan's father Frank Booth and colleagues, working in Karachi for BAC in 1950. Frank is centre front.

Travelling the world

My husband worked on Britannia, the Bristol Freighter, and he worked on Concorde in the laboratories for a while until he retired, but he travelled all over the world for them because he was a service engineer.

Audrey Hawes

Working at Bristol Siddeley Engines

As you get towards the end of an apprenticeship you look around for places to settle, and I quite liked what was called the Mechanical Research Department. It had an electronics area, engine control was done by analogue control systems; the new system called digital, or like computers, was just coming in. So the original controllers for things like the Concorde engines were analogue controllers, made by a company up in London called Ultra Electronics. I always felt these controllers had a limited future; the real future was these digital engine controllers, because you had much more flexibility in programming them, and could change the characteristics much more easily. I got involved in writing environmental specifications on the Concorde engines. We spent a lot of our time trying to get these controllers onto a suitable engine. We had proposals to get it onto the Concorde programme, but if they have got a tight time schedule, they don't want people messing up their programme. They saw us as a nuisance. You could change the GPDC, (General

A sales flight in the Bristol Wayfarer in the 1950s. From left: -?-, Alec Langfield, George Hawes, Jack Holt, Mrs Russell, Bill Pegg, Mr Russell, Captain Bartlett (Sales Director).

Purpose Digital Controller) you could change it to fit any engine, and any new engine that came along we tried to get these on, but it was hitting your head against a brick wall because Albert was not sympathetic to the new technologies. I think he saw us as a bit like some people would regard internet companies now. He saw us as just playing at engineering.

Albert, he was a boss of the old school, very much a character. One day he'd had some records out of a record library, and he'd brought these records in. We had these ovens for environmental testing, and he told someone to put these records in the ovens and put some weights on, because he'd left them out in the sun, and being vinyl they'd curved up. I don't know what it did to the acoustics, but when he took them back they looked perfectly good!

When I used to go back to university and meet up with other people, they were doing really interesting things. I had spent three months in the drawing office doing wiring diagrams, showing the connections from the instrumentation from the transducers down to the measuring instruments. Every so often they would do a change of wire; rub out one wire and put in another. It got really, really boring.

A chap called Fred used to say to me 'Tim, let's go for a walk.' The rule was you could walk anywhere as long as you could clutch a piece of paper, because if someone saw you with a piece of paper, they assumed you were on a mission, and they were scared about challenging you in case they got involved in the work. You could walk all the way around the factory clutching your piece of paper;

Tim Bowly, fifth from the right, in a group of electrical engineering students outside the Bristol College of Advanced Technology (which later became Bath University). The buildings are now the Brunel site of the City of Bristol College.

wander around the different flight sheds looking superior, because there wasn't the work there.

Concorde was going through, and I can remember the excitement because we were convinced it was going to be a great success. The provisional orders came in, but the fuel crisis of 1972 and the American opposition to Concorde, the spoiling tactics they adopted, I think killed Concorde as a truly commercial success.

I used to go to Whitchurch as part of the apprenticeship. They overhauled the engines for the Vulcan bombers, also the Centaurus and Hercules engines used for things like the Hastings, all piston ones. Every morning I got a bus down at the Arches, everyone smoking like mad – talk about secondary smoking! Gosh, I must have had a dose in those days. It was great, because young hands are a bit more agile. You used to be able to assemble the engines a bit quicker than they could, and they shared some of the bonuses with you.

You also had the bookies' runners. They'd put the bets in the bag, a timed bag, so once the bets had been put in they put a lock on it so that they knew the bets hadn't been placed after the race. I remember once we got this chap to explain how this locking system worked, and he locked his bag before anyone got the bets in! He was quite upset!

Tim Bowly

Progress chaser

I used to get in a lot of trouble because when the people on the shop floor were missing a part, I had to try and find it. When you went up to the office you were in between, taking all the flack. I suppose I enjoyed it, it was a job and I had to do something. I liked it. We were the No. 5 shop; the experimental shop, rather than production. I used to get into a hell of a lot of trouble between the people on the shop floor and the office; 'find the pieces', 'we want this piece', 'we don't know anything about it'.

Phillip Shield

The extensive overhaul and repair base at Whitchurch, Bristol.

BAC fire service

When I started there was just the one BAC brigade funded by BAC Aircraft, BAC Guided Weapons, Bristol Cars, Bristol Composite Materials, Bristol Siddeley Engines and the MOD for the airfield and the RAF site, although the RAF did have one small dry-powder unit for the training squadron. At one stage in 1965 there was four separate fire brigades at Filton. Bristol Aircraft Company had a full crew of about sixty-five, plus auxiliaries around the factories, Engine Division and Aircraft Division. You had BOAC, 'cos they used to rent part of the main Assembly Hall where they were working on Stratocruisers and Constellations, and they had their own fire brigade on the apron. You had the RAF fire service, because they were flying much bigger aircraft down here so they needed their own fire service, and you also had the Ministry of Civil Aviation Fire Service out at Filton as well. Apparently they never worked together, never exercised together, nothing!

The first big fire I went on was when the oil and paints store at Bristol Cars went up. We were on nights in 1967 and it was about midnight. We were all sat down in the rest room having a cup of tea. Mac, who was the leading fireman, had gone out and come rushing back in and said 'There's a big fire on top of the hill!' We'd had no phone calls. 'Oh, go away Mac,' we used to laugh like. He said 'Honest,' and we looked out the window. At the top of Filton Hill where Bristol Cars was, all we could see was this mass of flames going up in the air, and we still hadn't had a phone-call. We didn't know where it was – we just headed for this mass of flames. When we got there it was the oil and paints store going up at Bristol Cars. We fought the fire, but what we didn't know until a few days later was we were walking on this wooden floor, and underneath this floor there was forty gallon drums of white spirits, cellulose, and the ends were burning. In a few more seconds, if we hadn't cooled them down, goodbye. We would have lost two crews. It just would have blown, and we'd have gone with it.

The central fire station at the A38 end of the runway.

Robert Talboys in the fire station control room.

All the extinguishers were on site, that's something between 11,000 and 12,000 extinguishers that had to be serviced regular. Your hydrants had to be checked and painted, fire detection systems as they were coming in, evacuation systems, all had to be checked on a regular basis, and records made. Each department would have an evacuation drill.

We never went on strike. We always had this compensation from the unions not to strike. We would go in as normal, and we would stay on the station not doing any work other than your normal daily checks and lectures, but we didn't go out and service any extinguishers. The only time we would leave the station was if somebody called an emergency.

I was on duty on the day Concorde rolled out for the first time for press call. I stood by Concorde from the minute she drawed out for the morning 'til the time they put her back to bed at night, apart from a short dinner break on a number six. She was towed down to Cribb, a Concorde running-in base at the

Cribb's Causeway end of the runway, and backed into the detuners where all the Concordes would then do their engine running. I also stood by on the first test bed run for the Concorde engines. Whenever they ran a new engine for the first 'x' number of times, you had to have a crash tender standing by.

Robert Talboys

Diversity

I moved into the research department, and ended up doing environmental testing on weapons and aircraft. I used to be responsible for running a large chamber in which you could put a complete Bloodhound missile or part of a fuselage of an aircraft, and you could get this chamber up to 110°F with 99% humidity, and you could then pull it down through all changes of climate, including torrential rain, until we got it down to zero, and then take it on down to -60°F. Believe you me, at -60°F, you go in there wearing an electrically-heated suit, and if you touched the bare metal with your hand it would leave your skin stuck to the metal. On the Bloodhound launcher we were doing cold weather testing for Finland, and we used to get problems with the cutting and the shearing at very low temperatures on one of the drive motors. I'd have to go in there and change the coupling and a small circlip. You'd have to take your gloves off to do it so you accepted you'd lose skin.

We were doing testing on the Bloodhound launcher before it went into service, and one of them collapsed on me. It folded down into loading position with a missile on it, and I managed to roll into a ball in the one corner as it came down, otherwise I would have been squashed.

I thoroughly enjoyed working there, but if you looked at the environment compared to Health and Safety conditions now, it was bad.

Most people have gone deaf due to the noise of riveting guns. We would cut asbestos with no mask. We would be using paint without wearing a mask. You didn't think about it at all – it was just the conditions. The work climate was totally different, 'cos as working conditions went it was a good place to work and a very interesting place, cutting-edge technology all the time. There were things we were working with there forty years ago, only started coming on general use perhaps ten years ago.

The Alpha dinghy was designed by somebody at Oxford University in revolutionary glass-fibre reinforced plastic in the early 1950s. Nobody had the expertise to produce articles in this material apart from the aircraft industry. BAC had the contract to churn out the hulls, and this boat represents the very first production glass fibre sailing dinghy. We produced the hulls in Filton between 1953 and 1959. They were then sent to Oxford to be fitted out by the company that marketed them. And in addition they built two thirty-one-foot sailing cruisers in Plastics Division. I remember seeing those sailing in the Bristol Channel, and I believe the moulds were still in existence until not long ago in Bristol Composite Materials in Avonmouth.

Apparently BAC made beds at some stage; they ran a Housing Division. When the war ended the company had to diversify, and they went into all sorts of odd little schemes; prefabs, schools – there are at least two schools in Bristol still that were made in Filton, Lockleaze and Bedminster Down. The apprentices training college in Filton was BAC buildings until taken over by Filton College. They produced a chassis-less articulated lorry trailer; they produced sightscreens for cricket clubs. I worked when I was an apprentice on building an iron lung for use by polio victims. At the end of the war they built one motor torpedo boat with four Hercules aeroplane

A Bloodhound missile in the stratosphere chamber at Weybridge.

Geoff Lonsdale receiving a certificate in 1975.

engines in it, one driving each prop. Apparently it was the fastest MTB that had ever been built, with a noise level of 225 decibels in the engine room. By their very nature, air-cooled engines tend to be a little bit noisier than water-cooled engines. The Plastics Division produced bodies for the Lotus car; they also produced the body for a bubble car in the 1950s. This was a quite nice, quite elegant looking three-wheeled car called the Noble. Again, we used to subcontract for a German firm. We produced gun turrets; I worked on one contract for the Navy, turning Beaufort guns from manual drive to electric for ships.

Mike Jones

Danger, low flying kites!

When I started in the company I was in the drawing office. There was the fence, and then it was just wasteland, and then it was Charlton Road at Brentry, but they moved the fence and the gate miles out. The gate is now in Charlton Road. They built this new building, well, a couple of new buildings, on what was the wasteland.

There was a craze for making kites in the lunch hour; we used to get an hour then. We had access to great big sheets of paper and drawing material like paper but very strong, and people were making them bigger and bigger and bigger, and flying them in this wasteland. Eventually there was a stern warning from the air traffic control people. We had to stop because it was causing an aerial navigation hazard; all these great big kites flying about with aircraft taking off. All got stopped immediately.

Geoff Lonsdale

An inspector at engine division

I started at BAC in 1953, in the engine division, in the experimental department where all the new engines are built, developed and expanded. The development department (experimental) was a huge factory, because everything to do with the engine was done in the one building. Machine shop, fitting shop, inspection; 800 or 900 people working in one building. The earlier version of the Olympus, about the Mark 100, was being developed at that time. The first two engines were for a Canberra bomber, purely as a flying test bed, and it did actually set a new high-altitude record. As the engine was developed, different marks starting off with about 98 went to Mark 100, 101, 102, and 104. The engine becomes more powerful each time, eventually finishing up in the Vulcan bomber.

In Bristol there was two good places to work, and that was either BAC or Wills'

cigarette manufacturers in Bristol, the two big employers. Conditions were good, compared to other industries, but it was mainly the wages that attracted people. Very strong union, I think, stronger than what it is today. With your shop stewards, your own trade union membership was not compulsory, but the trade unions liked everyone to be in a trade union, and you were pressurised to a degree to join.

The way engines were developed; the whole concept changed over the years that I was there. When I started there first, the designers would design an engine on the old-fashioned drawing boards. The engine would be built to the designer's drawings and specifications, and once built would go to test, it would run for so long. Invariably there would be problems – it wouldn't reach the designed amount of power initially, so the engine would come back and be stripped. The engineers would come from their offices, inspect the engine parts laid out on the tables, note where the weaknesses were and suggest modifications. Parts would be modified, new parts manufactured, the engine rebuilt, bought back to test and it was all over and over again. There wouldn't just be one new engine, they'd build at least a dozen or so engines and they would go to test, testing different aspects of a particular engine. It would go on like that for several years, and eventually they would get the engine right and produce the power it was designed to produce.

They got these methods now where they can use 'spinning rigs', where they can test the service life of a turbine wheel. They can simulate ten years of engine life in a matter of weeks by taking the wheel, fitting dummy blade weights on the rim of the wheel to simulate the blades and mounting that on the end of a shaft inside a huge steel chamber. All the air would be sucked out of the chamber so they were running the disc in a vacuum, and there would be no friction because it's running in a vacuum. The shaft was

Phil Kirley at his workbench in the Experimental Inspection Dept, No. 4 shop at Rolls-Royce, c. 1989.

It was bitterly cold in February 1954 when George Hawes, aircraft engineer, was called out to the Bristol Britannia as she lay in the mud of the River Severn.

connected to a big generator, and would spin at quite a few RPM. It would rev up and down continuous, and they could simulate ten years' engine life in a matter of two or three weeks. And they had methods of testing individual blades on rigs by vibrating the blade.

Being new, and being in experimental areas, you always had failures. Like the time the Britannia went down on the mud flats. Now when that happened it was an engine problem, so we had all the engines back in the shop. Even the mangled bits, when they were failures, would be stripped and we would inspect the same as if it were a good engine. The failures laboratory could tell from examining the fractured pieces whether the fracture was a primary failure, in other word a material failure, or a design failure, or whether it was a secondary failure caused by damage. They could tell by just examining the fractured faces.

Phil Kirley

Working at Filton House, Head Office

The office was called Plant Records, and it dealt with incoming furniture and typewriters and all of it. I started as an office girl, and in those days you had to take all communications to wherever they had to go in the firm. There was no putting them in an 'out' basket to be delivered. I had to run about all over what we called Aircraft Works. We had to wear Quaker blue overalls, a complete whole overall. All the women had to wear these overalls, which were changed once a fortnight. There were three staircases in Head Office, and I used to wonder which staircase I would run up and down, because I was running up and down all day long. We weren't supposed to use the oval staircase, the best one, which came down to the main entrance where royalty used to come

The print room at BAC in 1948. Betty Beardmore is operating the print machine in the centre front.

in, but I did used to creep down there. We weren't allowed to use the three lifts – two passenger lifts and one goods lift – but we could use the goods lift when we were sixteen. We weren't allowed to use the other lifts until we were eighteen.

Come Christmas, I think we used to let our hair down a bit more, and I can remember we'd gone to the Anchor for a drink. I think I was a bit worse for wear. Coming back, I flung open the office door, and there was a cabinet behind the door with a typewriter on top with the carriage stuck out, and it was all glass doors of course, and the carriage went through it! I was told 'Miss Pearce, you are given to tomfoolery and buffoonery.' Oh, I did cop it. It was a wonder I didn't get the sack!

Betty Beardmore

Filton House dining rooms

I had had some training when I left school in a high-class restaurant, so when this job became available and they accepted me I was very pleased. Often we had VIPs, but we also

had the managers, and then the executives, the board of directors. They all had their different dining rooms. The South Room was used mainly for visitors, and the ordinary executives would dine with the visitors. There was the Managers Room; there was the Middle Room, as they called it, for executives; the next one was the board of directors', the most beautiful room of the lot. We had the Exhibition Room, which could also be used for special functions and downstairs on the next floor we had a huge Conference Room used for very big parties and functions, for something very special. In the beginning I had to work just as an ordinary waitress. I landed up in the directors' dining room where I stayed until I was promoted. The steward left, the supervisor took his place, and I took her place, but I had to learn a lot before I became a supervisor.

We had about fifteen staff. Then we had the chef who was in charge of his kitchen, an under-chef, a couple of ladies working in the kitchen, another lady on the dishwasher machine and a gentleman who came in and did the toilets and things like that. When I

Retirement celebrations for Steward Mr White in the 1970s. This gathering took place in the Director's Room in Filton House, with its walnut panelling and Chippendale chairs.

went there in the beginning Mr White was the steward, and he ran it like you would on a ship.

They had gardens in the beginning, and the gardeners used to bring the fresh vegetables to the dining rooms. Exotic fruits weren't in the shops out of season, but they would be ordered and flown over special; pineapples, melons, fresh strawberries, avocados. The grapes were always these beautiful bunches of black or green grapes, they were the best.

The board of directors' room – that was beautiful Chippendale. I think it was a walnut table, French polished, and the legs of the table they were sort of curved and they had brass lions on the bottom of the legs. The chairs were huge. The carvers on the end of the tables were bigger and they had armrests on, but the other chairs, enough for twelve people, they were slightly smaller, with beautiful wood carvings. There was a lovely antique sideboard where we used to put the bar and nuts and bits and pieces for the directors when they came in. The directors'

china was 'Napolean Ivy' bone china by Wedgewood, pattern number 4751, as used by Napolean at St Helena, 1815, in his exile; it was lovely. We had Stewart crystal on the table, with silver cruets. Everything had to be uniform, straight, in line, and the rooms had to be cleaned before and polished. A lot of spit and polish there. French doors led onto a veranda. There were flower beds, garden chairs and little wooden tables. In those days it was quite luxurious to have that kind of thing. The veranda had an awning all the way around to stop the wind, so they could sit out there and have their pre-lunch drinks, enjoy the view and talk. The floors were beautiful, parquet floors all the way through.

Sir Stanley used old Filton House. The boardroom there had Sir George White's photograph. When we took anything to Sir Stanley White, you always saw this imposing photograph of the first founder of the BAC. A coal fire was always lit for Sir Stanley, by the time he came in, sort of later in the morning. We did cocktail parties for the board of directors in their houses. One was called Mr Masterton; he lived in Clevedon and had a beautiful house there. Sir Reginald Verdon-Smith's house was on the harbour. I also served on his yacht. He was the yacht master one particular year, and he had three nights of cocktail parties for friends and people around Bristol. I went there and served cocktails and whatever from the house to the beautiful yacht. BAC had a guesthouse in Golf Course Lane where VIPs used to stay. We used to go up there from time to time and serve the evening meal. We were paid extra money like the factory; I think it was time and a third. If there was anything left, titbits and things like that, we were allowed to bring that home; smoked salmon rolls, asparagus with brown bread and butter, lots and lots of things. There was even caviar sometimes. My husband loved it if I was working late and came home: 'What have you got?'

The board of directors seemed to be very busy people. Sir Stanley White was very keen to sit down at quarter past one, and very often dined by himself because the others were away on business. Maybe once or twice a week the dining room would be fairly full, and then they'd sit together, but Sir Stanley always took the lead and they respected him very much.

We had to serve tea in the afternoons and coffee in the mornings for the offices, as well as get the lunch ready. Then in the afternoon a lot of the offices were used by managers and executives – we had to do a tray service. The trays were done up two together. You carried those on your shoulder. I only once slipped down with a tray; I walked into a ground floor room and slipped. I don't know what was on the floor, but my feet just gave way and bang, everything went on the floor. A bit embarrassing, but nobody got cross or anything like that. Mr Uwins, the director, the one who supposedly flown under the suspension bridge when he was younger, a bit of a daredevil, he was the one who always had

Earl Grey tea, and I took it down at quarter past three. That was the time he had to have it. I got right back up to the top of the building because he was situated in Old Filton House; we had lifts to go up to the top. I had only got inside the door and he'd rung up to say his tea was rather weak; I hadn't put any tea in the pot. So I had to make some more tea, go all the way back again, but he just smiled.

When the Duke of Edinburgh came, that was a very joyful occasion. It was wonderful to think he was coming; we were going to see him in the flesh. I did serve him; if you were a head waitress or a supervisor you always had the privileges, serving the main VIP visitor. Everything was planned to the last detail, and when he was coming out of the South Room going to the lift opposite, we were allowed to stand there, two or three of us, and wish him goodbye. He was very courteous.

The maiden flight of the Concorde, the first flight, we were allowed in the dining room, and they allowed us to open the skylight and go up on the roof and watch the maiden flight take-off. I found the envelope for the

On the balcony outside the Directors' Dining Room in the 1960s. Thelma Ryczko is on the right.

greetings telegram to Mr Trubshaw, the maiden flight congratulations. He left it on the table. He was sent that from Paris.

Thelma Ryczko

Inside Head Office

I worked in Filton House because we had to have some temporary accommodation while we had an office refurbishment a few years ago. The original directors' boardroom was all wood panelled with lovely ceilings. Out on the veranda, of course it's a very high point, the view is absolutely tremendous, all across the Cotswolds, absolutely super. The stairwell was one of these you could lean over the banisters and look right down and through, and all up one wall was a huge art deco stained glass window that had all the Bristol products like aeroplanes shown in the stained glass.

Geoff Lonsdale

A frightening experience in Canada

One major incident stands out in my past. I had a particular test to carry out on this day, being the NCO in charge of ground running and maintenance. I was told to fly with the duty pilot, and took the plane up on a test flight that turned out to be a quite horrendous experience.

We took off satisfactorily on frozen ice on the runway. I would accentuate here that we were flying in temperatures of approximately thirty-five or forty degrees below zero. That is about seventy degrees of frost [freezing point is 32°F above zero]. We took off satisfactorily, and had one or two minor incidents which corrected themselves, or that I was able to correct.

A stall test comprises getting to at least 12,000 feet, when the pilot then throttles the engines back gradually, until the aircraft drops out into a stall. Anyway, after this test, everything had appeared to be all right, and we shot off towards the British Colombia border, when we were suddenly wrapped up in a quite severe snowstorm. There was nothing but snow, and ice was building up on the leading edges of the wings. We had no such thing as de-icing equipment in those days; and anyway the pilot radioed back to base to say that we were coming in. It was then he discovered his magnetic compass, in fact both compasses, were malfunctioning. We had no radio functioning, we could raise no-one at all who could help us, so he said to me 'Dennis, we're in dead trouble here,' and I said 'You don't have to tell me, I thoroughly understand that, and I can't say I'm feeling very comfortable.' 'So anyway,' he said, 'I've got to go down,' and he went on again, down, down, down; then there was an absolutely horrendous crash. Propellers screamed to a seize, perspex and glass flew everywhere, the machine fell apart, and we were obviously held in by our safety straps. At that stage things did not look at all good for us.

I was now in a complete state of shock. My harness kept me secure, but my hands and face were scratched and torn by pieces of flying perspex and wood from the fuselage and the trees. There was nothing to be seen outside except trees, more trees, and masses of snow. I called to the pilot in his harness, slumped over the control column. I realised I had to do something. I looked at the pilot and he did seem to be in a bad way. I was suspended in my harness and could not put my feet on anything solid. It was freezing cold and there was that constant smell of petrol. I did manage to free myself from the predicament in which I found myself, and saw that the instrument panel and all the electrical switches were in the 'on' position. I immediately switched off.

After gaining my second wind, I scrambled down towards the tail end, and opened the first aid hatch and retrieved the Red Cross kit stowed inside. Using the contents to the best of my ability, I cleaned the pilot's head, applied some sterilised coagulant, and dressed the wound with a bandage.

After we'd found the S. and R. beacon, they did manage to get our position. After forty-eight hours some assistance arrived, and we were found to be a couple of dirty, scruffy, deplorable-looking individuals unfit to be seen in an RAF uniform! The pilot who had endured the unfortunate experience with me was later posted back to the United Kingdom to join Bomber Command, and we never made contact again. I myself became a member of Bomber Command when I returned home. I started with BAC Engine Division in I think 1954, in the buying department buying steel forgings and castings. You name it, I bought it. I was with the company for almost twenty-five years.

War is a strange business and at eighty years of age I am still here to tell this story.

Dennis Wiltshire FRAS, FAIAA, ARAeS, FIMgt, Hon RA.

Above: *Corporal Dennis Wiltshire of 80 Squadron RAF in 1940.*

Below: *Dennis Wiltshire at the launch of his book in February 2000.*

8 Brabazon and Britannia

The Brabazon was once the largest aircraft of its kind, but was axed by the Government soon after the prototype flew. Test Pilot Walter Gibb and local people recall their experiences of these aircraft.

The test pilot's story

I joined the Bristol Aeroplane Company, Engines Division, as an apprentice on 1 February 1937. Then the clouds of war were rolling over, and all my brothers and cousins were joining the forces, so I thought I would. I tried to join the RAFBR at the beginning of 1939 but it was full, so I put my name down, and it came up on 1 May 1940. I left the firm and went away to the war.

We really got on with things in those days. I had my first flying lesson on 29 July. By the time I went on Christmas leave I'd learnt to fly, got my wings, and been commissioned as a pilot officer, and was also a qualified instructor.

Wing Commander Walter Gibb, weary after his 1953 record-breaking flight in the Olympus-engined Canberra. Among the reception committee of managers and directors were George White and Reginald Verdon-Smith, joint managing directors.

A Bristol Type 170 Wayfarer freighter.

I think this is one of the main reasons why I'm alive today, because I'd been instructing for eighteen months before physically going to fight the war.

I joined a Mosquito squadron of night flyers, and worked my way up from Flight Lieutenant in 264 Squadron to Flight Commander in 605 Squadron, and then commanded 239 Squadron, an intruder squadron of Bomber Command, for the last nine months of the war.

When the war ended, I got a plum job as Wing Commander Flying at Defford, Malvern, the telecommunications flying unit for the radar establishments. I met various people at Filton through that, applied to come back, and they offered me a job as a test pilot. I came back on 1 April 1946. I had a very interesting career, because then we had the engines and the aircraft in the company, and had one flight-testing department for both. I took part in the development of three civil airliners – the Bristol Freighter, the Brabazon and the Britannia. And on the engine side, three prop jets: the Theseus, the Proteus and the Orion, and three jet engines: the Olympus, the Orpheus and the Phoebus.

They were a very interesting firm to fly for, because with a civil aircraft we used to do a lot of tropical trials, winterisation trials on various aeroplanes and sales tours. You went around and saw a lot of the world. One of the best tours I did was in a Bristol Freighter, when we flew all round Africa for six weeks. We had two days off for maintenance in Johannesburg, and during that time we did 122 hours flying and only changed one tail wheel and one spark plug in the engines. The Bristol Freighter was an absolutely first-class five ton lorry of the air.

The Brabazon, people say that it was a white elephant, and it was too, but it was a first-class aeroplane and it was a great achievement for the Bristol Aeroplane Company to get that aeroplane into the air in 1949. The only trouble was that the specification was wrong, and the airlines didn't want an aeroplane that big at that time. It was very advanced technically; it had the engines geared together, the propellers constant speeding, automatic synchronisation and reverse pitch airscrew braking, a 100% power control, no manual reversion and no mass balances. And it all worked! The Brabazon was a very nice

A Bristol Type 167 Brabazon.

Bristol Type 175 Britannia.

aeroplane to fly, and we did 400 hours development on it, of which I did more than half. By this time I had been made Assistant Chief Test Pilot, Bill Pegg's deputy, and we virtually flew it alternately. I did all the long flights.

Then we got to the Britannia, and that's an aeroplane that grew. First of all it was started off as the Medium-Range Empire, to replace the flying boats on the Empire route to Africa and right to Australia. Then they changed

their minds and put the Proteus in it. Then they thought it would do the Atlantic, so they extended it and put bigger engines in it, and it became an Atlantic airliner, and actually was the first aeroplane to do the Atlantic both ways. It's easy to fly from New York to England because it's downwind, but the other way is very difficult because you're into a headwind the whole time. We proved it for BOAC and the world in general by doing a non-stop flight, which I did, from London to

The record breaking Olympus-engined Canberra on the runway at Filton.

Vancouver. Took us fourteen hours and twenty-two minutes, a very interesting flight for me indeed.

The development of the Britannia took rather a long time, because we came across a new problem. In the inter-tropical front this aeroplane flew above 25,000 feet, which pistons hadn't done before, and the air intake for the engine was at the back, so the air had to turn round through 180 degrees in the air intake, and that used to get clogged up with snowballs. We didn't know this at the time. We had to do a lot of testing to see what the real problem was, because the engine used to bang, rather like a car backfiring, and occasionally used to stop. We used to go down to Entebbe on Lake Victoria, in the middle of Africa, flying in these clouds. We only understood really what happened when we had closed-circuit television in the air intake, and we could see the stuff building up. By putting little jets at the back of the air intake, which kept the snow moving, we cleared it all, and had no further trouble. And actually, the nice thing was it was a very good aeroplane.

Flight testing the engines; we had a lot of various aircraft to test them in, because you never wanted a new engine in a new aeroplane all at once, so we had things called flying test-beds, where we put one of our engines on to test it. The initial testing of the Olympus was done in a Canberra. The engines were taken out, and the aeroplane modified for two Olympus'. We did a lot of very high flying development on this, up to 55,000 and 60,000 feet regularly, because the engine was designed for the Vulcan Bomber. And with this we also had attempts at the altitude record, which we got, twice. We took all the weight out of the aeroplane. For every pound we took out, the aeroplane went nine inches higher!

At the end, the observer was taken out, and his ejector seat, so I was by myself. The first time we got the altitude to 63,700 feet I think it was, in 1953. Then two years later, 1955, the engines were bigger and more developed, and we got up to 65,890 feet.

It was a really 'hot rod' to fly. Because the aeroplane was designed for two Avons producing 7200lb of thrust, and in the end we had two Olympus giving 14000lb of thrust each we really had to watch it. It could achieve its critical Mach number at 50,000 feet on one engine, so you had to be careful. When we went to fifty-five and above we used

The Bristol Review - *the in-house magazine of the Bristol Aeroplane Company, celebrating the achievement of the world altitude record in 1953. This was also marked by the naming of a new road in Filton – Canberra Grove.*

partial pressured suits, because if pressurisation failed, they were really life jackets; you couldn't breathe up there, and you had only two seconds to live.

When all the mergers took place I stayed with the aircraft company and was made Service Manager. After that I went to Australia and was Managing Director, and six months later, Chairman and Managing Director of British Aerospace (Australia) Limited, until I retired at the age of sixty-five.
Wing Commander Walter Gibb, DSO, DFC, JP

Flights of the Brabazon

I helped break up the Brabazon, and then moved on to the very first Britannia as they were just coming on line. Only one Brabazon flew; the other one's main fuselage had been finished. It was built for a pre-war market, in the style of Imperial Airways, and didn't carry very many passengers. It was a beautiful aeroplane, designed with two decks, sleeping quarters, cinema and a lounge. By the time she should have been finished, times had changed and people wanted to fly cheaply in

not so much comfort. I saw its maiden flight. Up on the golf course we had a perfect bird's-eye view of the runway, and we saw take-off from there. Huge plane and very, very majestic, very slow because it was so big. It seemed to hang in the sky and had an unmistakable noise from the eight engines, very distinctive, very droning.
Mike Jones

Bill Pegg takes off

We saw the big hole they were digging to build those hangars; there was trucks gliding everywhere. I remember it being carved out of the hillside. When the Brabazon took off everyone was aware of it. It was a lovely sunny Sunday morning. I was out in the back garden, and you could hear the noise of eight Centaurus engines revving up. Bill Pegg was apparently halfway down the runway, when he realised he was doing eighty miles an hour and lifted off, he didn't really intend to take off, it was only a taxiing drive. I remember it climbing up and flying around. We were in Station Road, and it flew around and landed again, just went one circuit and landed. It was quite an experience for all the people in Filton at that time. It was scrapped because it was too big and too slow.
Ken George

Enormous

Once we saw the Brabazon fly right over Bristol, and the thing that struck us was that it's very large, and going very, very slowly and very noisily. I think though that it was higher than it seemed because of its enormous size. We often saw the prototypes for the Concorde flying over Filton. We just used to wave at it.
Frances Blandford

The majesty of flight

I was there the day the Brabazon flew for the first time. It was the most exciting day because he wasn't meant to fly, he was meant to just taxi along the runway.

Bill Pegg, Chief Test Pilot, taxied along the runway and we were all watching this huge, vast, aeroplane – it seemed enormous. Well, it was enormous. It taxied along the runway, and as we watched, so it just lifted, so slowly, so grandly, majestic. And the cheers that went up from people! We all went up onto the golf links to watch it, because that was a perfect view. It was nothing like jet aircraft; it just sort of ambled down onto the runway, and ambled along the runway. It was so slow and so majestic that it was unbelievable – nothing like Concorde coming in and landing and taking off.

Audrey Hawes

A contrast in size

Mrs Breens: We went on the golf links to watch the Brabazon. Arthur, our son, was only about two, and he wondered why they were so small against the big plane.

Mr Breens: We looked down onto the airfield, and there were tractors down there, and Arthur said 'Someone's left their toys out!'

Mr and Mrs Breens

I saw the Brabazon fly

I was in my pushchair being pushed along Doncaster Road in Southmead when the Brabazon flew low overhead. My mum held me up and said 'There you are, when you're a man you can tell people that you've seen the Brabazon fly.' I don't pretend to remember!

Geoff Lonsdale

Charlton, a village that died

Mum had friends that lived in the Charlton village, and they had this beautiful Tudor house. It got pulled down, the whole village. They moved her from there and she came to live in Fairlawn Avenue. I was sat there one day and she said to me 'Did you ever see the painting that George White had done for Betty?' [her second daughter], and I said 'No.' She took me into their front room, and she walked straight to the window, and she said to me

The Bristol Brabazon on show at the Bristol Aeroplane Company's Families Day in June 1950.

A roof fire at the Brab Hangar.

'There it is there. I can't look at it.' She just couldn't look at it.

Hilda Saunders

Building the hangar

The next major thing was when Charlton Village was demolished, and the Brabazon runway and the assembly hall for building the Brabazon aircraft was built. That was quite a major works, because over the Filton hill where the golf club is now, you could walk all the way down that field, until you came to the railway line going from Parkway now down to Henbury and Avonmouth through the tunnel at Charlton. All that earth was scooped out to build the hangar!

John Buckley

The Brabazon hangar – a huge cathedral!

7.30 a.m., in the dark, walking through the back corner. There'd be hardly any lights on, and there's just echoing black space with just a few odd lights, and gradually the odd light would click on; nothing, no noise but the hiss of the air lines. Then suddenly a drill would start up, and then a riveting gun, and the whole place would gradually come to life and it was superb – it was like a huge cathedral. In many respects the hangar's an even more outstanding achievement than the Brabazon, because the Brabazon used almost existing technology, whereas that hanger – nothing had been built that size.

Mike Jones

The hangar architects

We had a contract at the garage to supply petrol. We supplied it to William Press and Son, who were the major constructors and contractors, and we also supplied the architects. Brian Calhoun Associates were the people who designed the building, and used to call and see how the work was coming on. While he was looking at the works, the chauffeur who drove the Rolls-Royce brought the car round to the garage and filled up with petrol, and parked the Rolls-Royce on our forecourt which was very good advertising for the garage. He would get out his duster and polish and polish up the Rolls-Royce. He'd be there until the telephone went, and Mr Calhoun would ask him to come round and collect. A Rolls-Royce filling up with petrol used to take about fifty gallons. To sell fifty gallons of petrol, when our average sell was four gallons of petrol, was quite an event at four and sevenpence halfpenny a gallon. When a Rolls-Royce pulled in and filled up the tank with nearly half as much petrol as you had in your storage tank, it was quite a thing.

John Buckley

Working on the Britannia

On Britannia, all the rivets were heat-treated, so they became soft while you put them in. Then over a period of time they were what was known as age-hardened to regain their strength. This heat treatment consisted of immersing them in a bath of molten salt, after which they were taken out, put in the refrigerator, and they would stay in this softened state for a period of three or four days. When you went to do any riveting you went to stores, drew your rivets (handed out to you in a coloured tin), say red first thing in the morning, and red last from 7.30 to 9.30

a.m. There were coloured lights in the hangar as well, and at 9.30 a.m., a klaxon would sound, and the red light would go out and a green light would go on, and at that point you dropped whatever you were doing, took what was left of your red tin of rivets back to the stores, and drew the appropriate colour again and started riveting. If after that time you were caught with the wrong colour tin, all the rivets you had to put in that morning would be taken out because they couldn't be guaranteed that they wouldn't crack.

Mike Jones

Interior fitting

I went into the RAF, came out and went to work for a while at Longwell Green Coach Works. One of the fellows who worked at the tramway with me said 'My father-in-law works for George Parnalls – they want people there to work on the Britannia on interior furnishings.' George Parnalls in Fishponds on the causeway were high-class shop fitters. They did all the big stores in London and all over the world. They did out ships as well, so that's where I ended up. I worked there for eleven years, starting on the shop floor. I eventually became charge hand, and then into the lofting, setting out, and eventually into the drawing office. It was sub-contracted because they had the skills, the machinery and the wherewithal to make all the interior furnishings. I would go out with three or four fellows, and we might have to fit a bar unit or a toilet unit, and you had to do it in a certain time. If the aircraft was on flight test, you went with the aircraft and flew around and worked while they were testing the aircraft 'cos they had to get the hours in for flight approval. It was a very interesting life, you know. You had to put the best in; it would be rejected by the Air Inspection Department if it wasn't right. We did interiors for BOAC, North American,

Bristol 175 Britannia.

Midwestern; they all had their own different designs obviously, and colour schemes, different logos, different positioning of furniture. Parnalls had the flexibility to design it and make those changes because they were experts in their field.

Keith Trott

The seasons

I remember that we tended to get more severe winters there when we were working in the Assembly Hall. If an aircraft needed to be moved on a winter's morning – you used to get a lot of fog there – all the hangar doors would open, and immediately the whole hangar would fill with fog. They'd move an aircraft, close the doors again, and you had the whole hangar still filled with fog for twenty minutes or a good half-hour afterwards. When it snowed, because there was a large bank running up to the golf course, we'd get sheets of aluminium and go sledging in our lunch hour. We'd all sledge down the bank, get soaking wet, and then we'd have to get behind the heaters at the side of the hangar and dry our clothes before we could start the afternoon shift.

In midsummer, on a plane the size of Britannia there would perhaps be thirty or forty people working in there. There were no fluorescent lights – we all had filament lead lamps in those days – no fume extraction, and a lot of people would be using Evo-Stick. You could cut the atmosphere with a knife in there, but nobody got high – you just got a splitting headache. You'd have to go outside, get a breath of fresh air, and get back on the job again 'cos all the time you weren't working you were losing bonus.

Mike Jones

9 The Space Programme

Filton had an important role in the nation's space programme, contributing to the development of projects such as GEOS, the Hubble space telescope and Giotto. Here, Mike Goose records some of that history.

I came to Filton in September 1952, doing an apprenticeship at what was then the Bristol Aeroplane Company. After six months in the training workshop, the first job I had was to help cut Brabazon up into little bits.

About three-and-a-half years into my apprenticeship, I moved into a testing laboratory, which dealt almost entirely with guided weapons. I then worked on guided weapons for many years, up through to the mid 1970s.

The problem with guided missiles is that they were made and then perhaps not used for many years, and they work only once. You fired them and that was the end of it, so you had to try and ensure that even though you'd built them many years before, and trundled them about all over the world, and they'd been subjected to all sorts of different climatic conditions, when you pressed the button, they worked. So that was really the purpose of the environmental test laboratory, which had lots of climatic chambers, salt chambers, dust chambers and vibration machines and so forth.

I drifted into the space programme, largely because of this environmental test activity. Spacecraft in a way are similar to weapons, in that they're subject to very severe vibration on the launcher, and high levels of acceleration. Then in space they're subject to a vacuum, and extremes of temperature. If the spacecraft isn't in sunlight it will go down in temperature towards -200°C, and if it's in sunlight without any thermal control it will go up to very hot temperatures, certainly higher than the temperature of boiling water. So you have to test for these things because once you've launched them, you can't get at 'em.

The few cases where you can get at spacecraft since the days of space shuttles are the lower orbit machines, like the Hubble space telescope. These are only at an altitude of a couple of hundred miles or so, but space shuttle can't go any higher than that. A lot of spacecraft, the geo-stationary ones, that appear to be stationary above the earth's surface, are at a height of 20,000 miles, so they're really not 'get-at-able' after launch.

My first encounter with spacecraft was in the mid 1960s. There was a programme called Black Arrow, a purely British programme; British launcher and British spacecraft. They built three spacecraft carrying various experiments to do with magnetic fields and so forth. It was launched successfully in Woomera, but then was cancelled. Since then, Britain has not had a stand-alone programme. My involvement was when it came into the environmental test laboratory for the vibration testing. It went elsewhere for the thermal and vacuum testing because we didn't have those sorts of facilities in those days.

The other early involvement with space-related activities was with Skylark sounding rockets, rockets about half a metre in diameter and twenty metres in height. They would go up to an altitude of 150 miles or so, but they were simply up and down devices. They spent eight or nine minutes in weightless conditions, and they carried various experiments. The first one was launched in about 1957, and they went through to about 1990. We launched about 412 with very few failures.

The next real spacecraft we got involved with were the early UK satellites, mainly concerned with measurement of magnetic and electric fields. UK 3 and I think UK 4 were built at Stevenage, and there was then a UK 5 and a UK 6 which were built at Filton. This coincided with the contract from Hughes Aircraft in America to help build INTELSAT 4, which was a geo-stationary communications satellite. There was no design involved as far as I remember. It was just the manufacture, testing various bits and pieces, but it was a huge satellite and pulled us into the twentieth century.

The first big satellite that we designed and built was a machine called GEOS. This was also concerned with the measurement of magnetic and electric fields, and what we were trying to find out about was the interaction between the sun's magnetic and electric field and the earth's magnetic and electric field, because as the earth travelled round the sun, it produced something much akin to the wake on a ship – there's a bow wave and there's a wake trailing out behind. This was of great interest to the scientists. The problem was that the levels of magnetic and electric field we were trying to measure were extremely low. So the spacecraft had to be made non-magnetic. All the equipment on the spacecraft couldn't be allowed to produce electric or magnetic fields, which would interfere with the experiments. I got involved, because at that time I was still working in the environmental test laboratory. All the units on the spacecraft, the various power supplies, the controllers and the altitude and orbit control systems and so on had to be tested. There were dozens of them, and the spacecraft assembly and integration team really didn't have the experience of testing lots of units, and I did.

One of the first buildings appearing on what is known as Twenty Site was an assembly building for the INTELSAT 4 satellite, and a round thing called the gasholder. The gasholder was where we operated. The reason for the gasholder was that we were looking for this very quiet magnetic and electric field environment, and one of the chaps went and lowered his instruments into a gasholder at Eastville, and found it was very quiet, so one was built of our own. The problem is that everything electrical produces an electric field and a magnetic field as well. Since the turn of the last century, the electrical environment (what's around us) has increased millions of times. That's what I mean by quiet, because out in space, out over 20,000 miles, the levels of magnetic and electric fields were very low, very much lower than occurs around us on earth. So the problem was to prove that these sensors would measure these low levels, when in fact they were sat on earth at higher levels.

I then went quite successfully through the whole of the GEOS programme, the environmental system test programme. This was mostly done abroad, at the European Space Agency in Holland or in the magnetic facility in Munich, and that took something like eighteen months.

We went to America to launch it. Unfortunately the American launcher went wrong. It launched the satellite but it put it in entirely the wrong orbit. The scientists got some interesting data out of it, and it was considered in the circumstances to be successful. There was certainly nothing wrong

GEOS Satellite.

with the spacecraft. The spacecraft did everything it was asked to do. Anyway, the European Space Agency was persuaded that we should build another one, as we'd got a number of spare units. So the first one became known as GEOS 1, and was launched in April 1976. We built another one called GEOS 2, and it launched in July 1978.

In parallel with all this we were involved in a job to develop a solar array. The solar arrays are the solar cells that either attach round the outside of the spacecraft, or some of them come out on wings, which provide the electrical power to the spacecraft. The problem is, of course, that on the top of the launcher, you can't stick great panels of solar arrays outside the launcher. They have to be folded up and made compact, and then when the spacecraft gets into orbit they have to come out. Someone had the brilliant idea that one way of doing it was somewhat like a roller

blind. You stick the solar cells to a flexible substrate, and then you roll it up in a tube. Then, in space, you have a mechanism to roll it out. We were involved in an early sort of feasibility contract, where we built one of these things and tested it, and that in fact led us on to building the solar arrays for the Hubble space telescope.

The other thing we developed and built for the Hubble space telescope was called the photon detector assembly, a very low light camera that, as the name suggests, actually detects and counts photons, particles of light. The simple explanation of this performance was that if you set it up on earth, it could see a candle flame on the moon. The pictures it has produced since, of galaxies and so forth on the edge of the universe, have been absolutely amazing. That was a very small instrument. I guess it was not much bigger than two-thirds of a metre long, and twelve or thirteen

GEOS Satellite under construction. Mike Goose is on the right.

centimetres in diameter, but it was cutting-edge technology. That was built at Filton.

In Europe, all the spacecraft activities are organised under the European Space Agency. Most of the European countries are members, and they contribute an amount of money every year. The way the system works is that they supposedly get out from the various projects work to the value they've put in.

All these European space projects are collaborative. One country would provide the structure, another the power supply, another the reaction control system, another the attitudes and orbit control system. Then, one country, and this was the thing that we prided ourselves on doing well, was to put it all together.

After GEOS, which is perhaps in the public's eye the most notable thing, came the idea of building a spacecraft that would go and have a look at a comet. Why don't we build a GEOS 3, and aim it at a comet, and see what comets are made of? Nobody really knew much about them. This went through many trials and tribulations; in fact, the spacecraft ended up not looking at all like GEOS, other than it being of similar size. This spacecraft was called GIOTTO.

The spur to getting on with it was Halley's Comet. Halley's Comet was well known, and in a highly predictable orbit. Time was fairly limited; I think it was about four years or so to start off, get on with it, and to launch. The project was successful; the spacecraft was launched on 2 July 1985, and it encountered the comet in March 1986. The spacecraft was, in effect, in orbit round the sun, and the orbit was so designed that it crossed the path of the comet as close as possible. It was known that comets emitted a stream of particles and dust ahead of the comet, as well as the more visible tail, and it was not known what damage this dust would do, because if I remember correctly, the spacecraft was approaching the comet at something like 70,000 miles per second, so that even microscopic dust particles had high energy. The spacecraft was equipped with two bumper shields. The theory was that a particle hitting the front bumper shield would vaporise, and the bumper shield behind it caught the vapour. It was successful to an extent. The spacecraft actually worked to within a few seconds of its closest encounter, and then contact with the spacecraft was lost.

The spacecraft was wobbling, and of course it was a very long way away, so that it lost radio contact with earth. But the spacecraft had an in-built autonomous guidance system designed, if it was disturbed like that, to re-acquire the earth, and in fact some hours later it did so. And there were still bits of the spacecraft working. The camera had been blasted to bits by these fast particles, but a surprising amount of the spacecraft did work, and in fact it was the decided to send it to another comet. The comet was called Grigg Skjellerup. Giotto was put into hibernation, and then went in its orbit round the sun. With difficulty it was reactivated, and it went and encountered this second comet in July 1992. By then it had been going for seven years.

In the meantime, things were changing at Bristol. There was always lots of reorganisation of the aerospace industry in general, and in 1982 we were put together with the Hawker Siddeley people at Stevenage to become one company, which was looked upon with some trepidation. In actual fact it worked very well. Stevenage expertise was in communications spacecraft, both military and civil, whereas our line of business had always tended to be with scientific spacecraft. Stevenage had far too much work. They had been very successful in getting work for communications spacecraft, and we were able to help them out. We built some of their spacecraft for them, like SKYNET and NATO, which were purely military communications satellites. They also built things like MARECS, a maritime communications satellite. In fact you'll often hear on the news, perhaps when a ship has been in trouble, they have made contact by MARECS satellite. If you go on a cruise and you telephone somebody at home, that communication is through a MARECS satellite.

One of the advantages of this new grouping was that where previously we'd been scattered through ten or more bits of buildings, we now managed to build our own office block. It was called the Halley Building (in connection with Giotto), which opened in 1985. Then another huge building (which in fact was built for a secret project which was cancelled) was opened in 1986, and we then used it for several programmes. We needed that building, which had a huge assembly hall, because we got involved with a project that was initially called Columbus Polar Platform. This was a spacecraft associated with the International

The roll up solar array. Mike Goose is back left.

Space Station, but is a quite separate spacecraft. It's about the size of a single-decker bus, and it carries various experiments to observe the earth's surface. It can take pictures, it can measure the height of the sea, it can look for various resources and it's in a polar orbit. In other words, it goes round the earth from pole to pole and the earth rotates underneath it. It's going round every ninety minutes, so over a period of time it covers the whole earth's surface.

I did not see the first build of this vehicle. I left in 1993, but the programme was completed and launched, and it's now called ENVISAT, short for Environmental Satellite. It was interesting because the other day there was a programme on television about giant waves, thirty metre waves, which sea captains had reported. Apparently the world merchant fleet loses one ship a week, not perhaps entirely due to these waves, but that's one of

Celebrating Giotto.

the contributing factors. The scientists said that from their mathematical calculations these waves were impossible. However, some other scientist using quantum mechanics proved that they were possible. Someone had the bright idea of using the sensors in ENVISAT to look for these waves, and sure enough, it produced pictures of about ten of them in a very short time. That's the sort of thing it can do, mapping, looking for resources, checking the height of sea level, those sorts of things.

The question was asked how it was decided what we would do, and why we would do it, and how these particular programmes were chosen. The early programmes, Black Arrow and the UK series of satellites, were largely UK government-funded. There were various scientific institutions, universities, who were working on astrophysics, and earth environment and so forth, who wanted information and managed to persuade the powers that be to put up the money. The sounding rocket programmes were largely driven by the need for various academics to get information. The European Space Agency (ESA), a European collaborative organisation, was initially entirely driven by science. Various European universities wanted information about the environment, and were able to persuade the ESA that this was the way to go. The ESA encouraged member governments to fund these sorts of activities. There was a general theme of science running through these things, and there was a bit of heart-searching in the late 1970s and early 1980s as to whether the European Space Agency should get involved with manned programmes – in other words, whether they should put up astronauts. The UK government was always very against manned programmes. They're terribly expensive, and in general the European Space Agency took the same line. The French were very keen to have a manned programme but they really couldn't find the support elsewhere in Europe.

The need for communication satellites was driven by the fact that the business was dominated by the Americans with their Early

Bird and INTELSAT series spacecraft, and they were making a lot of money. The ESA started off with some European communication test satellites. The first one was called OTS, or Orbital Test Satellite. These were just put up, and time was given to the member countries to put out test transmissions and develop their ground stations. These developed into European Communications Satellites (ECS), built on a commercial basis. They relayed television, radio and telephone communications, and people paid to use them. Another system was developed entirely for maritime communications traffic called MARECS – Maritime European

Communication Spacecraft. The British military have their own communication satellites called SKYNET, and a similar system was produced for NATO, which just enables the services to communicate. All these spacecraft are geo-stationary. They sit above one point on the earth.

So that brings me very quickly up to when I left Filton, and almost up to the present day. Unfortunately, the space business at Filton largely disappeared a couple of years ago. There was a merger with Marconi, and Matra in France, and as far as I know there are no longer spacecraft building activities at Filton.

Michael Goose

Intelstat IVA communication satellite due for launch in 1975. BAC manufactured the subsystems.

10 The Bristol Car

After the war, BAC diversified into various fields in order to retain skilled workers, and use some of the capacity no longer needed for the war effort. Bristol Cars, started in 1945, moved to larger premises in the former Shield Laundry building when it became vacant in the 1950s. In 1960, car production briefly returned to the aircraft factory before finding a permanent home at Patchway. The cars have become a byword for excellence in motoring. Tony Crook and colleagues tell the story.

The development of Bristol cars

During the war, while in the RAF, I started a company called Anthony Crook Motors, which dealt with all sorts of sports cars, mostly being the sales and servicing outlet at the time. That coincided with Bristol's starting up. So Bristol Cars (which was then part of Bristol Aeroplane Company) and Anthony Crook Motors ran alongside each other. In 1960, the government of the day said there were too many aircraft companies getting subsidies, so Bristol Cars could have departed then, but the grandson of the founder (Sir George White) and I bought the car company and ran Bristol Cars together until his nasty car accident in 1969. I became more and more involved, until he retired altogether in 1973. At one stage we were going to have a Bristol Siddeley car, with an Armstrong Siddeley engine.

The original Bristol car

I've still got the first car. It was absolutely marvellous. We took the best of BMW, given to us in 1945 for war reparations from the BMW factory. We flew over and took what we wanted, all the plans and so on. We completely re-engineered it – people say it was a 328 BMW engine, which it wasn't, but that doesn't matter. It was completely re-engineered, and that was a great achievement, because if you look at it, it really was one of the first post-war cars, although it had leanings in pre-war.

The Chrysler connection

By a strange coincidence we met Chrysler's directors. One of my activities, as well as Bristol Cars, was importing a French car called Simca. Chrysler suddenly decided to make the Simca not far from our head office in London. I was still racing, so when the directors of Chrysler came over and said 'Put Tony Crook in a Simca and take it around Brands Hatch,' this was just a bit of fun. We went back to Kew to have lunch, and outside was my Bristol. The Bristol Aircraft Company was making a very light 3.8 litre engine, but we hadn't got a gearbox. Chrysler's directors came out after we'd had lunch and said 'lovely motor.' I said 'A bit of a difficulty because the gearbox was being made in another factory that burnt down.' They said 'Why don't you try one of our gearboxes?' So they sent the gearbox over, and attached to it was a Chrysler engine. Sir George looked absolutely horrified, but I said 'We'll stick it in a chassis and test the gearbox like that.' The car went extremely well, so that was the start of our forty-year plus alliance with Chrysler. That was another milestone, going from our own engine to a very big engine. It went even more quickly and still had a very good fuel consumption.

'Firsts' at Bristol

There were lots of 'firsts' at Bristol. We invented a special seat belt that is on all cars now. If you look at BMWs and Aston Martins, when you open the door the window goes down slightly, and then up again, and that was my invention. Another milestone came in 1976: we were the first to make cars run on liquid petroleum gas (LP) and petrol. And now, within a few weeks, we have a car in here running on LP from new, not a conversion. Instead of filling up for fifty pounds you can do it for twenty-five pounds. We were the first British company to turbocharge cars; we don't do that anymore. That's fifty-seven years since it started. We've had lots of milestones and we're still at it!

Bristol cars – present and future

What we have now is the Blenheim. In a few weeks that will come out again, looking the same, but with this dual fuel thing. And then we are making a 200mph car, which is a departure for us, because in the mid-1950s we made a 404 car. We only made fifty of those, and they were supplementing the larger car. As the very wealthy people took Blenheims

Sir George White, when he and Tony Crook bought the Car Division in 1960.

away, they said 'Why don't you make one of those?' I said 'Well, I don't think we could compete with little MR2s.' Well, they didn't mean that, they meant Maclarens and Aston Martins. So we will make a small run of those; a maximum of twenty a year. It should have started now, but deliveries will start in January 2003. That will be £200,000, which is a hell of a lot of money, but it is a third of the price of the Maclaren.

The first car was registered in 1946, so that's fifty-six years ago, and it is absolutely essential that we shall never leave this area. The lease goes on for another twenty-five years. So we've got all the facilities here.

A line up of Type 400 cars awaiting delivery to customers, outside the Filton factory in 1948.

Bristol cars – exclusive and discreet

Over the years, many famous people (one of the very early scoops was Stewart Granger and his wife Jean Simmons) became very friendly with me because a lot of people used to follow me around the racing tracks. We sold them two cars – of course, that created an enormous thing. There were people like the British heavyweight champion Don Cockell; he used to come with me to Goodwood. They'd say 'Tony Crook has got his minder and he wants a decent handicap!' More recently, we have got some of the top pop people of the day, and of course Bristols are sold everywhere. You can't say what type of person owns a Bristol. The car's never been an old man's car; it's been a car that people couldn't achieve until they had got on a bit further. There is a spectrum of everybody, from cabinet ministers to just anybody, you never know who is going to buy a car.

Travelling from Kensington to Filton – by plane!

When we were right bang in the middle of the airfield, my boast was that I could be in the Kensington office, which is in the High Street, drive to White Waltham Airfield on the other side of Heathrow, and be in my office on the Filton Airfield within an hour. You couldn't bloody well do it in anything else! When I started in the 1940s and the 1950s you couldn't get through Kensington to Filton in anything less than five hours. I used to fly up and down, two hours total there and back at the outside instead of a whole day. When the motorway came, that cut the time down, but it was still quicker in the aircraft to go back and forth. Now when I fly into Filton, they radio ahead when I will be arriving and collect me from here, which is five minutes. I used to fly to see suppliers all over the country. We could use farms strips and take people there; we used to take stores up and down. When we delivered new cars up to London, instead of all the business of getting on a train and so on, you just nip them up in the aircraft and then come back again. We've got two aircraft, and if you use those enough, like we did do, then it's not expensive.

Bristol cars – what the future holds

I owned the company with Sir George from 1960-1973, and then I owned it completely from 1973 onwards. People say 'I don't suppose you will go on forever.' Unlike my cars I'm not indestructible, so some years ago we had investors come into the company, and my successor is now the chairman of the company. I shall go on until I drop, which could be any minute! The company is in very good hands and will go on in private ownership. We are the only British-owned luxury car manufacturer. In the days when there was Rolls, Aston, Jaguar, they were all independent. Then Rolls and Bentley went to Germany and Jaguar went to Ford. We are still autonomous, and we stand alone. People ask if that has helped us. In fact, when Bentley and Rolls went, people used to come in the showroom and say 'I really forgot that you made cars,' because we play it so quietly. And orders really started to go up.

How to keep your skilled workers and exclusivity

Right from the very beginning, even in the aeroplane company days, we said we would limit the number of cars to 150 a year. When we started making cars at the end of the Second World War, there were literally 50,000 people working at Filton, and there wasn't the business there was during the war making Blenheims, Beaufighters and so on. So Bristol Cars was started with a small number made per week. When Sir George and I took over

Tony Crook in 1960, when he and Sir George White became the owners of Bristol Cars.

in 1960, now and for the future, we just like to make slightly fewer cars than people want to buy. Like this, we can keep the nucleus of the workforce. I'm particularly grateful for some of the people who have trained up. Simply from a financial point of view there's not this roller coaster where people go out of business. I've seen Jensen go several times, people like that. You make more cars and leave them in fields, or make fewer cars than they want, and keep exclusivity, and you've got survival and some form of future.

Car number one

I'll tell you something about car number one, and the very first Goodwood. In 1948, Goodwood track was opened, and the old Duke of Richmond opened the track with car number one. Fifty years later in 1998, Goodwood re-opened, and young Lord Charles, his grandson, rang up and said: 'Tony – you have still got the car. Can I open up Goodwood again with it?' So Goodwood was

A car of the Bristol Blenheim series taken next to a Bristol Blenheim fighter aircraft from which the car took its name.

opened in 1948 with car number one, and Goodwood was opened in 1998 with car number one.

They put all the old Grand Prix drivers in cars as near as possible to what they drove, but I was the only bloke who had still got the very car. The only thing I've done to that was to decarbonize it with my own fair hands. When we were going around the track, me sitting with Lord March, I said 'You can go as fast as you like.' He said 'Won't it break?' 'No, No,' I said. We did another lap, and I said 'Look at the speedo– 350,000 miles.' The jackpot of one Bristol car, a two-litre engine, was in fact 600,000 miles with a vet in Scotland.

Tony Crook

A career with Bristol Cars

I was in the war for six-and-a-half years. When I was demobbed, I knew a friend of mine was working here, a manager at the time, so I applied for a job. I got the job and worked here ever since. I've been on supervision since 1951, when I went on the staff. I've designed all the cable harnesses up to the present model. During my time with Bristol Cars we did sub-contract work. We were wiring up the Britannia aircraft leading edges; we had quite a few people on that. We were also making gun turrets as well, on a sub-contract basis. I used to have thirty-four people working on that job.

My greatest moment was when we produced the 450 racing car. I used to work during the daytime doing the normal work, and in the evenings I would work on the 450 doing all the electrical work. It was my pleasure to go out in the first one on the runway at six o'clock in the morning, with a gentleman by the name of Dave Summers. He designed the 450, and it was a wonderful experience. That was the highlight of my time here. It has been a pleasure to see every model made, and it's a pleasure to drive these cars; I enjoy driving at fast speed. If a car is crashed, I go to the workshop in London and estimate,

JHY 261 on the left is the very first Bristol car made in 1946. Known as the Type 400, this actual car is still owned by Tony Crook.

One of every Bristol car made from the company's inception in 1946 until 1955. From the left: Type 450, class winning, Le Mans sports car; Type 405 drophead; Type 405 saloon; Type 404 short chassis two seater; Type 403 saloon; Type 402 convertible; Type 401 saloon; Type 400 saloon. All the cars, including engines and gearboxes, were made at Filton. The photograph was taken in front of the Brabazon Hangar doors.

and then I supervise the repairs down here. We do all the body repairs and paintwork here. The people in London specialise in the mechanical work, but I still have fitters to do mechanical work in the local area. We have several customers, and they come here rather than go up to London. It's a very well organised company.

Syd Lovesy

The lasting appeal of a 'Bristol'

I've just always loved the cars. I think it's a very English idea; it costs a lot of money, it's wonderful to be in and drive, but it doesn't make any show of it outside. I think that people who have good taste and the money to indulge themselves, like that.

Tony Crook in the Cooper Bristol with Syd Lovesy in a Bristol Blenheim.

They're not being looked at – only they know how good it is.

It doesn't get unwanted attention; in fact most people don't even know what it is. People are very polite when you drive it. I'll often drive something else in, and I wonder why people are being so mean to me, and it's the reaction to the car. I'm so used to people reacting well to the Bristol. It's a car that does absolutely everything you'd want. It sometimes saddens me when I see someone who is maybe sixty years old, and they are down at the service department taking their car in for the first service, and they say 'This is the car I've always wanted, and I just didn't realise it was here.' It seems a shame that they've had to wait 'til then. Fortunately, most people who are buying the cars are surprisingly young, which is a great sign for us. The average age on the cars is probably in the middle to late forties, which is a lot younger than traditionally people like Rolls-Royce and Bentley have been. We have people who are very young who've had them for years. It's a nice spread of age, but it's not one type of person. What people tell us is that the car does what a traditional sports car like an Aston Martin would do, but equally, in comfort terms, it does what a traditional Rolls would do. It's not too big, it's not too ostentatious, and it's a really good car to own. It's a very fast car. There are two models; the Blenheim 3 and the Blenheim 3S, which is relatively newer, a higher performance engine. In practice, the Blenheim 3S is as fast as anything you'll come across on the road, but doesn't look it. In today's world that's not a bad thing. But there's virtually nothing that is faster in terms of a four-seat car, or handles better. With the Blenheim you can take four people, you can put a lot of luggage in, and you can drive to the South of France in a day very comfortably. The car does so much more than you would imagine it does, and it does pretty much everything you would want in one car. It really makes us proud when you look in London and there are people who have got twenty cars, but the car they put their parking permit on is the Bristol, because that is the car they use every day. They could drive anything, but that is what they chose to drive, because it's the car that is most useful, and most enjoyable for them day to day.

It is not at all uncommon to see a Bristol that is thirty or forty years old being used everyday. Most classics, they're really not

Cars being produced in the Filton factory in the mid-1950s.

usable day to day, whereas a Bristol is. It's nice to see people actually out using them. People rally them, they take them to work everyday; they're very, very usable old cars. And my father has a 1975 Bristol 411; he often takes it on rallies. It's quite amusing, you find someone in a modern Porsche, and you're actually pushing them along in a thirty-year-old saloon Bristol, it does a lot more than you'd realise from looking at it.

I think Mr Crook and I are really doing it because we love the cars, and I think other manufacturers are doing it because it's a business, it has to make money. It has made money over many years, but at the end of the day, I suppose you should say we are both in love with the cars!

Toby Silverton

Only the very best!

I can remember when I was the order clerk; we used to send to Michelin for the tyres and Kidderminster for the carpets for them and things like that. It was all the very best stuff that went into the cars.

Sylvia Johnson

A wonderful ride

On one occasion I was privileged to be put in a Bristol Car, and driven just down from Filton to Patchway. It was like floating on a cloud. Wonderful, it really was.

Audrey Hawes

Contributors

The authors would like to acknowledge and thank the following for the use of their photographs:

Filton Library: photographs on pages 10, 16 (top), 17, 22, 29, 53, 59, 105, 112, 115, 119; John Hutton: pages 12, 26 (bottom), 54, 55, 56 (three pics), 57, 58, 76; Tony Crook, Bristol Cars Ltd.: pages 121, 122, 123, 124, 125 (two pics), 127; Irene James: pages 40, 41, 42 (top), 43, 45, 46, 48; Hilda Saunders: pages 11, 18, 26 (top), 31, 52, 106 (top); Stan and Jackie Sims: pages 13, 35, 69, 75 (top), 104, 109; Phillip Shield and Maureen Lomas: pages 9, 20, 68, 87; Ken George: pages 42 (bottom), 47, 62, 89, 107; Mike Goose: pages 96 (top), 116, 117, 118; Robert Talboys: pages 38, 94 (two pics), 110; Thelma Ryczko: pages 101, 101; Sylvia Johnson: pages 25, 30; Betty and Peter Beardmore: pages 33, 34, 90; Rodney Hewett: pages 44, 71, 72; Audrey Hawes: pages 60, 91, 98 (bottom); Britton Family: pages 73, 79, 83; Brian Richards: pages 16 (top), 17, 29; Mary Lake: page 70 and frontispiece; Cliff Price: pages 24, 84; Frances Logan, Margaret Tarr: pages 27, 90; Jane Tozer: pages 75 (bottom), 85; Mr and Mrs Breens: pages 81, 82; Dennis Wiltshire: page 103 (two pics); Mr Baker: pages 4, 106 (bottom); Tim Bowley, page 92; John Buckley, page 19; Joan Dando, page 65; Filton People, page 64; Mr and Mrs Hall, 67; Hobbs Chemist, page 39 (bottom); Mike Jones, page 37; Phil Kirley, page 98 (top); Syd Marks, page 28; Mrs Monks, page 14; Colin Pulsford, page 23; Phyllis Sutton, page 77; Keith Trott, page 49; Sue and Geoff Lonsdale, page 96 (bottom); Ann Churches/Reg Clegg, page 61; South Gloucestershire Aviation Website, page 39 (bottom); Emergency Fire Service, Marchington, page 51.

Permission to reproduce Copyright photographs, kindly granted by:
Filton Camera Club: for photographs on pages 16 (top), 17, 29.
Bristol Evening Post/ Western Daily Press/ Bristol Evening World: for photographs on pages 22, 40, 42 (top), 46, 48, 60, 73, 83.
Gloucestershire Gazette: for photographs on pages 31, 45.
Rolls-Royce: for photographs on pages 93, 94 (two pics).
AIRBUS UK, BAE SYSTEMS: for photographs on pages 4, 39 (bottom), 63, 88, 91, 96 (two pics), 99, 100, 104, 105, 106 (two pics), 108, 110, 112, 115, 116, 117, 118, 119.